CW01022955

Table of Contents

1

Dedication

I am dedicating this book to my Three Daughters Lynn, Bethany & Jennifer who have fulfilled and enriched my life so much! Your combined spirits and hearts are generous and beautiful. You are my link to life and the continuity of life, and of love.

Preface

This book will assist parents and adults alike with the "Language of Today" which includes common text messaging, acronyms as well as common emoticons and similes that our kids, teenagers and adolescents that own mobile devices use today to communicate among each other.

This book provides and understanding and knowledge of the art of texting, SMS, Online Chatting and etc. of the certain acronyms, texts, and emoticons used today for their daily communications today. Though the material in this book describes definitions, acronyms and emoticons kids use every day, it is also general enough for parents newly assigned to the world of wireless texting. It can also be an excellent accompaniment to a short seminar and training class.

DON'T TEXT & DRIVE:

Researchers found out that; the study showed that drivers who text and drive become more than one third slower than if they were coherent and not texting – this was compared to a person at the DUI limit or under the influence of illegal drugs. Text messaging lowered reaction time by 35 percent, while people high on marijuana slowed down 21 percent and those who were drunk slowed down by 12 percent.

"Put down the phone...or be accident prone"

"Stay alive...don't text and drive"

What You Can Do

Give Clear Instructions – Give teen drivers simple, clear instructions not to use their wireless devices while driving. According to Cellular Telecommunications Industry Association, the easiest way to say it is: "On the road, off the phone." Before new drivers get their licenses, discuss the fact that taking their eyes off the road – even for a few seconds – could cost someone injury or even death.

Lead by Example – Children learns from their parent's behavior. No one should text and drive. Be an example for your children and if you need to text or talk on the phone, pull over to a safe place.

Become Informed and Be Active - Set rules for yourself and your household regarding distracted driving. Tell family, friends and organizations to which you belong about the importance of driving without distractions. Take information to your children's' schools and ask that it be shared with students and parents.

Marc G. Leclair

Common Text Messaging & Chat Abbreviations/Acronyms

Text message abbreviations come into play when users try to compose a complete message in only 160 characters. Over time, wireless users developed their own lingo, but many common text message abbreviations are unfamiliar to those who are just getting started with texting. Sending text messages is fast replacing standard cell phone conversations when it comes to communicating information quickly, and learning the following text

4

message abbreviations can save you even more time. If you have ever received a text message or text-based online chat message that seemed to be written in a foreign language, this book Texting & Online Chatting "The New Language of Today" Quick list of text acronyms and emoticons will help you translate the chat lingo by providing the definitions for text message acronyms.

With the popularity and rise in real-time text-based communications, such as smartphones, tablets, Facebook, Twitter, e-mail, Internet chat rooms, and mobile phone text messaging (SMS), came the emergence of a new language tailored to the immediacy and compactness of the new communication media.

While it does seem incredible that there are thousands of chat and text message abbreviations, remember that different chat abbreviations are used by different groups of people when communicating via mobile and/or online. Some of the following chat abbreviations may be familiar to you, while others may be foreign because they are used by a group of people with different online interests and hobbies than your own. For example, people playing online games are likely to use chat abbreviations that are different than those used by someone running a financial blog or updating their Twitter status.

This set of chat guides offers definitions and translations for Text Messaging & Chat Abbreviations Twitter, SMS, and Facebook, emoticons and smiley face abbreviations.

Disclaimer: You may see a little profanity but I feel it's better to be informed than to be ignorant. Many of the acronyms and emoticons below are universal and are used even where the native language is not English.

"Numbers & Characters"

? - I Have A Question and/or I Don't Understand What You Mean

?^ - Hook Up?

?4U - I Have A Question For You

?RUD - What Are You Doing?

! – I Have A Comment

,!!! – Talk To The Hand

*$ - Starbuck

*$$ - Starbucks

;S - Gentle Warning, Like "Hmm? What Did You Say?"

^^ - Meaning "Read Line" and/or "Message Above"

<3 - Meaning "Sideways Heart" (Love, Friendship)

</3 - Meaning "Broken Heart"

<33 - Meaning "Heart or Love" (more 3s is a bigger heart)

@+ - At Plus

@TEOTD - At the end of the day

.02 - My (or your) two cents worth

0773H - Hello

1TG, 2TG - Meaning number of balls needed for win

1040 - You owe me big time

1174 – Nude Club

121 - One-to-One

1337 - Leet, meaning 'elite'

143 - I love you

1432 - I love you too

143444 - I love you very very much

14AA41 - One for all, and all for one

182 - I hate you

19 - Zero hand

10Q - Thank you

10X - Thanks

1CE - Once

1DR - I wonder

1i – One Eye

1NAM - One in a million
2 - Meaning "to" in SMS
20 - Meaning "location"
22 – TuTu
24/7 - Twenty-four hours a day, seven days a week
262 - Old
26Y4U - Too sexy for you
2b - To be
2B or not 2B – To be or not to be
2B@ - To Be At
2BZ4UQT – Too Busy for you cutie
2C - Too cool
2C4U - Too cool for you
2D - To delete
2day – Today
2DFM - Too dumb for me
2EZ - Too easy
2FB - Too F***ing bad
2G2B4G – Too good to be forgotten
2G2BT - Too good to be true
2G4Y - Too good for you
2H2H - Too hot to handle
2M2H - Too much too handle
2M2M - Too many too mention
2MFM - Too much for me
2MI - Too much information
2MORO - Tomorrow
2NITE – Tonight
2nt – Tonight
2U2 - To you too
2ZDA - Tuesday
303 – Mom
360 - I love you back and/or right back at you
3RZDA – Thursday
3sum - Threesome

4 - Short for "for" in SMS
404 - I don't know and/or I haven't a clue and/or Page not found
411 - Meaning 'information'
420 - Let's get high and/or "Marijuana"
458 - I love you
459 - I love you (ILY is 459 using keypad numbers)
4AO - For adults only
4AYN - For all you know
4COL - For crying out loud
4E - Forever
4EAE - Forever and ever
4eva – Forever
4ever – Forever
4GM – Forgive Me
4got – Forgot
4MTK - For Me to Know
4n - Foreign
4NR - Foreigner
4OTS - For old time's sake
4Q – F*** You
4rl – For Real
4sale – For Sale
4U – For You
4U2 - For you too
4ward - Forward
4YEO - For your eyes only
^5 - High-five
511 - Too much information (more than 411)
53X – Sex
555 - Laughing
55555 - Crying your eyes out and/or meaning laughing
5FS – 5 Fingers Salute
6Y – Sexy
747 - Let's fly and/or we're leaving

7K – Sick
8 – Ate and/or Oral Sex
81 - Meaning Hells
831 - I love you
86 – Over/Out of, and/or over, and/or to get rid of, and/or kicked out and/or we are outta here
88 - Bye-bye and/or Hugs & Kisses
8TB - Ate the bait
9 - Parent is watching
99 – Parent no longer watching
s - Meaning "smile"
w - Meaning "wink"

"Letter A"
A – Hey
A-OLS - Administrators On-Line
A/S/L - Age/sex/location
A/S/L/P - Age/Sex/Location/Picture
A2T - Addicted to texting
A3 - Anytime, anywhere, anyplace
AA - Alcoholics Anonymous and/or As Above and/or Ask About
AAAAA - American Association against Acronym Abuse
AAF - As a matter of fact and/or As a Friend and/or Always and Forever
AAK - Asleep at keyboard and/or Alive and Kicking
AAMOF - As a matter of fact
AAMOI - As a matter of interest
AAP - Always a pleasure
AAR - At any rate
AAR8 – At any Rate
AAS - Alive and smiling
AATK - Always at the keyboard
AAWC - After a while crocodile
AAYF - As Always, Your Friend

AB – Ass Backwards
Ab/abt - About
ABC - Already been chewed
ABCP - A bad computer professional
ABITHIWTITB – A bird in the hand is worth two in the bush
ABS - ***hole Behavior Scale
ABT – About
ABT2 – About To
ABTA - Meaning Good-bye (signoff)
ABU - All bugged up
AC - Acceptable content
ACC - Anyone can come
ACD - ALT / CONTROL / DELETE
ACDNT - Accident (e-mail, Government)
ACE - Meaning marijuana cigarette and/or Access Control Entry
ACK – Acknowledge
ACORN - A Completely Obsessive Really Nutty person
ACPT - Accept
ACQSTN - Acquisition
ADAD - Another day, another dollar
ADBB - All done, bye-bye
ADD - Address
ADDY - Address
ADIH - Another day in hell
ADIP - Another day in paradise
ADM - Ay dios mio
ADMIN - Administrator
ADMINR - Administrator
ADN - Any day now
ADPIC - Always Dependably Politically Incorrect
ADR – Address
ADVD - Advised
AE - Area effect

AEAP - As early as possible
AF - April Fools
AFAGAY - A Friend as Good as You
AFAHMASP - A Fool and His Money Are Soon Parted
AFAIAA - As far as I am aware
AFAIC - As Far as I'm Concerned
AFAICS - As Far As I Can See
AFAICT - As Far As I Can Tell
AFAIK - As Far As I Know
AFAIR – As Far as I Remember
AFAIU – As far as I understand
AFAP – As far as possible
AFAIUI - As far as I understand it
AFC - Away from computer
AFDN - Any F***ing Day Now
AFFA - Angels Forever, Forever Angels
AFGO - Another F***ing Growth Opportunity
AFIAA - As Far As I Am Aware
AFINIAFI - A Friend in Need Is a Friend Indeed
AFJ - April fool's joke
AFK - Away from keyboard and/or a free kill
AFN - that's All for Now
AFPOE - A fresh pair of eyes
AFU - All f***ed up
AFWIW - Anyway, for what it's worth
AFZ - Acronym Free Zone
AGB - Almost Good Bridge
aggro - Aggression
AGKWE - And God Knows What Else
agl - Angel
AH - At home and/or Auction House
AHFY - Always here for you
AI - As if
AIAMU - And I am a Monkey's uncle
AIGHT – Alright

AIH - As It Happens

AIMB - As I Mentioned Before

AIMP - Always In My Prayers

AIP - Agreement in Principle

AIR - As I remember

AISB - As it should be and/or as I said before

AISE - As I Said Earlier

AISI - As I see it

AITR - Adult in the room

AIUI - As I Understand It

AKA - Also known as

ALAP - As Late as Possible and/or as long as possible

ALIWanIsU - All I Want Is You

ALCON - All concerned

ALOL - Actually laughing out loud

ALOrO - All or Nothing

ALOTBSOL - Always Look On the Bright Side of Life

ALTG - Act Locally, Think Globally

ALYWING - Acting like you're working

AM - Antemeridian

AMAP - As much as possible and/or As many as possible

amazn – Amazing

AMBL - All my boundless love

AMBW - All my best wishes

AMF - Adios Mother F***er

AMG - Ah my gosh

AML - All my love

AMOF - As a matter of fact

AMRMTYFTS - All My Roommates Thank You for the Show

AMS - Ask me something

AMT - Actress-Model Type

ANFAWFOS - And Now for a Word from Our Sponsor

ANFSCD - And Now for Something Completely Different

ANGB - Almost Nearly Good Bridge

AO - Anarchy Online
AOAS - All of a Sudden
AOB – Abuse of Bandwidth
AOC - Available on cell
AOE - Area of effect
AOI - Ass on ice
AOM - Age of majority and/or Age of Mythology
AOMM - Always on my mind
AON - Apropos Of Nothing and/or All or nothing and/or As of now
AOR – Agency on Record
AOTA - All of the above
AOYP - Angel on your pillow
AP – Apple Pie and/or Attached Parenting and/or Attack power
APAC - All praise and credit
APAS – As possible as soon
APM - Actions per minute
APP – Application and/or Appreciate
AQAP - As quick as possible and/or quiet as possible
AR – Action Required
ARE - Acronym rich environment
arp - Armor penetration
ART - Assuming Room Temperature
AS - Ape Sh** and/or Another Subject
ASIG - And so it goes
ASAFP - As Soon as F***ing Possible
ASAMOF - As a Matter of Fact
ASAP - As soon as possible
ASAT - As simple as that
ASAYGT - As Soon As You Get This
ASL - Age/sex/location
ASLA - Age/sex/location/availability
ASLMH - Age/Sex/Location/Music/Hobbies
AT - At your terminal

ATAB - Ain't That A Bitch
ATB - All the best
ATC - Any Two Cards/Automated Teller Machine
ATD – Agree to Disagree
ATEOTD - At the end of the day
ATF - Asshole Toleration Factor
ATM - At the moment
ATPM - About to pee myself
ATSITS - All the stars in the sky
ATSL - Along the same line (or lines)
ATST - At the Same Time
ATT - All the time
ATTN - Attention
ATW – All the Web and/or Around the Web and/or All The Way
ATWD - Agree That We Disagree
ATYS - Anything you say
AUNT - And U Know This
AUNTM - And U Know This Man
AUT - Are you there
AV - Audio Visual
AWA - As well as
AWC - After a while crocodile
AWESO – Awesome
AWGTHGTTA - Are We Going To Have To Go Through This Again
AWHFY - Are We Having Fun Yet?
AWL - Always with love
AWLTP - Avoiding Work like The Plague
AWNAIC - All We Need Is another Chair
AWOL - Absent Without Leave and/or Absent while online
AWT - At what time
AWTTW - A Word to the Wise
AWTY - Are we there yet?

AYC - Aren't You Clever and/or Aren't You Cheeky and/or Are You Coming?

AYCE - All You Can Eat

AYFR - Are you for real

AYK - As You Know

AYKM - Are you kidding me?

AYOR - At Your Own Risk

AYPI - And your point is?

AVPWIP - Are you pondering what I'm pondering?

AYS - Are you serious? and/or Are you stupid?

AYSOS - Are You Stupid or Something?

AYST - Are you still there?

AYT - Are you there?

AYTMTB - And you're telling me this because

AYV - Are you vertical?

AYW - As you were and/or As you want and/or as you wish

AYWK - As you well know

azm - Awesome

AZN – Asian

"Letter B"

B – Back and/or Be

B& - Banned

B&F – Back & Forth

B/C – Because

B/F - Boyfriend

B/G - Background (personal information request)

B2W - Back to work

B4 - Before

B4N - Bye for now

B4U - Before You

B4YKI - Before You Know It

B8 - Bait

B9 - Boss is watching

BA - Bad ass

baa – Bad and/or Not good
BaBitsU - Baby It's You
BABY - Being Annoyed By You
BAC - Bad Ass Chick
BAF - Bring a friend and/or Being a Friend
BAG - Busting a Gut and/or Big Ass Grin
BAK - Back at keyboard
BAMF - Bad Ass Mother F***er
BANANA - code word for penis
BARB - Buy Abroad but Rent in Britain
BAS - Big ass smile
BASOR - Breathing a sigh of relief
BAU - Business as usual
BAY - Back at ya
BB - Be Back -or- Buzzard Breath and/or Bebi / Baby (Spanish SMS)
BB4E – bye, bye forever
BB4N – Bye, Bye for Now
BBAMFIC - Big Bad Ass Mother F***er In Charge
BBB – Bye, Bye Babe -or- Boring Beyond Belief
BBBG – Bye, Bye Be Good
BBC - Big bad challenge
BBFBBM - Body by Fisher, Brains by Mattel
BBFN – Bye, Bye for Now
BBIAB - Be back in a bit
BBIAF - Be back in a few
BBIAM - Be back in a minute
BBIAS - Be back in a sec
BBL - Be back later
BBM - Brains by Mattel
BBMFIC - Big Bad Mother F***er In Charge
BBN - Bye, bye now
BBQ – Barbeque and/or Be Back Quickly
BBR - Burnt Beyond Repair
BBS - Be back soon

BBSD - Be Back Soon Darling

BBSL - Be Back Sooner or Later

BBSS - Be back soon sweetie

BBT - Be back tomorrow

BBW - Big Beautiful Woman

B/C - Because

BC – Because and/or be cool

BCBG - Bon Chic Bon Genre and/or Belle Cu Belle Geulle

BCBS - Big Company, Big School

BCDHM - Be careful, don't hurt me

BCNU - Be seeing you

BCO - Big crush on

BCOS – Because

BCOY - Big crush on you

BD - Big Deal and/or Baby Dance and/or Brain Drain

BDAY - Birthday

B-DAY – Birthday

BDBI5M - Busy Daydreaming Back in 5 Minutes

BDC - Big Dumb Company and/or Big Dot Com

BDN - Big damn number

BEG - Big evil grin

BF – Boyfriend and/or Brain Fart and/or Best Friend

BF2 - Battlefield 2

BFAW - Best friend at work

BFD - Big F***ing Deal

BFE - Bum F***ing Egypt and/or Best friends forever

BFFL - Best friends for life

BFFLAB - Best friend for life and beyond

BFFLNMW - Best friends for life, no matter what

BFFN - Best Friends for Now

BFFTTE - Best Friends Forever Til the End

BFG - Big freaking grin

BFN - Bye for now

BFO - Bald, fat, and old and/or big, fat and old

BFR - Big F***ing Rock

17

BFU - Bald, fat, and ugly and/or big, fat and ugly

BG - Big grin

BGWM - Be gentle with me

BH – Blockhead and/or Better Half and/or Bloody Hell

BHAG - Big Hairy Audacious Goal

BHIMBGO - Bloody Hell, I Must Be Getting Old

BHL8 - Be home late

BHOF - Bald Headed Old Fart

BI – Business Intelligence and/or Bad influence

BI5 - Back In Five

BIB - Boss is back

BIBI – Bye, Bye

BIBO - Beer in, beer out

BIC - Butt in chair

BIF - Before I forget

biffles - Best friends for life

BIH - Burn in hell

BIL - Brother-In-Law and/or Boss Is Listening

BIMD - Back in my day

BIO - Bring It On

BIOIYA - Break It Off In Your Ass

BION - Believe it or not

BIOYA - Blow It Out Your Ass

BIOYE - Blow It Out Your Ear

BIOYIOP - Blow It Out Your I/O Port

BIOYN - Blow it out your nose

BIT - Bitch in Training

BITCH - Basically In the Clear Homey

BITD - Back In the Day

BITFOB - Bring It the F*** On, Bitch

BITMT - But in the meantime

BJ – Blow Job

BKA - Better Known As

BL - Belly laugh

BLBBLB - Back like Bull, Brain like Bird

BLNT - Better luck next time
BM - Bite me
BM&Y - Between Me and You
BME - Based on my experience
BMF - Bad Mother F***er
BMGWL - Busting My Gut with Laughter
BMHWB - Be my hot-water bottle
BMOC - Big Man on Campus
BMOF - Bite Me Old Fart
BMOTA – Bite me on the Ass
BMS - Baby making Sex
BMW - Burly Mountain Woman
BN - Bad news
BNDN - Been Nowhere Done Nothing
BNF – Big Name Fan
BNR - But not really
BNSCD - But now something completely different
BO - Bug Off -or- Body Odor
BOB - Back off buddy and/or Battery Operated Boyfriend
BOBFOC - Body off Baywatch, Face off Crimewatch
BOCTAAE - But Of Course There Are Always Exceptions
BOE - Meaning "bind on equip"
BOFH - Bastard Operator from Hell
BOHICA - Bend Over Here It Comes Again
BOL - Best of luck
BOLO - Be on the look out
BON - Believe it Or Not
book - it means cool
BOOMS - Bored out of my skull
BOP - Meaning "bind on pickup"
BOSMKL - Bending over smacking my knee laughing
BOT - Back on topic and/or Be on That
BOTEC - Back Of the Envelope Calculation
BOTOH - But On The Other Hand
BOYF - Boyfriend

BPLM - Big person little mind

BR - Best regards and/or Bathroom

BRB – Be Right Back

BRBB - Be Right Back Bitch

BRNC - Be Right Back, Nature Calls

BRD - Bored

BRH - Be right here

BRS - Big Red Switch

BRT - Be right there

BS - Big Smile and/or Bull Sh** and/or Brain Strain

BSAAW - Big Smile and a Wink

BSBD&NE - Book Smart, Brain Dead & No Experience

BSEG - Big Sh** Eating Grin

BSF - But seriously folks

BSOD - Blue screen of death

BSTS - Better safe than sorry

BT - Bite this and/or Between technologies

BTA - But Then Again and/or Before the Attacks

BTAIM - Be That As It May

BTD - Bored To Death

BTDT - Been there, done that

BTDTGTS - Been There, Done That, Got the T-shirt

BTFO - Back the F*** Off and/or Bend the F*** Over

bther - A bit under the weather

BTHO - Back the hell off

BTHOM - Beats The Hell Outta Me

BTHOOM - Beats the Heck Out Of Me

BTHU - Back the hell up

BTM – Bite Me

BTN - Better Than Nothing

BTOIYA - Be There or It's Your ass

BTOBD - Be There or Be Dead

BTOBS - Be there or be square

BTSOOM - Beats the Sh** Out Of Me

BTTT - Back To the Top and/or Bump to the Top

BTW - By the way
BTWBO - Be There With Bells On
BTWITIAILWU - By the Way I Think I Am in Love with You
BTWITIAILWY - By the way, I think I am in love with you
BTWITIILWY - By the way, I think I'm in love with you
BTWITILY - By the way, I think I love you
BTYCL - Meaning 'Bootycall'
BU&I - Between you and I
BUBU - Slang term for the most beautiful of women
BUFF - Big Ugly Fat F***
buhbye – Bye
bup - Backup Plan
BW – Best Wishes
BWDIK - But what do I know
BWL - Bursting with laughter
BWO - Black, White or Other
BWQ - Buzz Word Quotient
BWTM - But Wait, There's More
BYE - Response to BYE?
BYKT - But You Knew That
BYOA – Bring your own Advil
BYOB - Bring your own beer
BYOBB&B – Bring your bed, broad, & booze
BYOC - Bring your own computer
BYOP - Bring your own paint
BYOW – Bring your own wine
BYTM - Better you than me
BZ - Busy

"Letter C"

c ya – See ya

C&G - Chuckle & grin

C-P – Sleepy

C-T – City

C/P - Cross Post

C/S - Change of Subject

C2C - Cam to cam

C4N - Ciao for now

C9 - Parent in room

CAAC - Cool as a Cucumber

CAD - Control + Alt + Delete and/or Short for Canada/Canadian

CADET - Can't Add, Doesn't Even Try

CAM - Camera (SMS)

CAS – Crack a Smile and/or Clothing Acquisition Syndrome

cata - Cataclysm

CB - Coffee break and/or Chat Brat and/or Chat Break and/or Crazy Bitch and/or Call Back

CBA - Can't be ass

CBB - Can't Be Bothered

CBF – Can't Be F***ed

CBJ - Covered Blow Job

CC - I understand and/or Carbon copy and/or Crowd Control

CD9 – Parents are watching

CD99 - Parents are no longer watching

CDIWI - Couldn't do it without you

CF – Coffee Freak

CFD - Call for Discussion

CFS - Care for secret?

CFV – Call for Vote

CFY - Calling for you

CHA – Click Here Asshole

Chingo - Chat lingo

chx - Chicken

CIAO - Good-bye (Italian word)
CIBM - Could it be magic?
CICO - Coffee in, coffee out
CICU - Can I see you?
CICYHW - Can I Copy Your Home Work
CID - Crying in disgrace and/or consider it done
CIL - Check in Later
CINBA - Clad In Naught but Air
CIP - Cell it please
CIR – Children in Room
CIS - Consumer Information Service
CLAB - Crying like a baby
CLM - Career Limiting Move
CM - Call me
CMAP - Cover my ass partner
CMB - Call me back
CME - Checking my e-mail
CMF - Count My Fingers
CMFWIC - Chief Mo Fo of who's in charge
CMIIW - Correct me if I'm wrong
CMON - Come on
CMU - Crack Me Up
CNP - Continued (in) next post
CNRHKYITF - Chuck Norris roundhouse kick you in the face
CO - Conference and/or Company
COA - Course of action
COB - Close of business
COBRAS - Come On By Right after School
COC - Code of conduct
COD - Change of Dressing
COFR - Cry out for revenge
COH - City of Heroes
COL - Crying out loud

COS – Child Over Shoulder and/or Change of Subject and/or Because

CP - Chat post and/or Cross Post

CPE - Coolest Person Ever

CPF - Can pigs fly?

cr - ChatRef.com

CR8 - Create

CRAFT - Can't remember a F***ing thing

CRAP - Cheap Redundant Assorted Products

CRAT - Can't Remember a Thing

CRAWS - Can't Remember Anything worth A Sh**

CRB - Come right back

CRBT - Crying really big tears

CRD - Caucasian Rhythm Disorder and/or Deficiency

CRIT - Meaning "critical hit"

CRS - Can't remember sh**

CRTLA - Can't remember the three letter acronym

CRZ - Crazy

CS – Career Suicide

CSA – Cool Sweet Awesome

CSG - Chuckle, snicker, grin

CSL - Can't stop laughing

CSS - Counter-Strike Source

CSThnknAU - Can't Stop Thinking About You

CT - Can't talk

CTC - Care to Chat and/or Contact and/or Choking the Chicken and/or Call the Cell

CTFO - Come the F*** On

CTFU - Cracking the F*** up

CTHU - Cracking the hell up

CTMQ - Chuckle To Myself Quietly

CTN - Can't talk now

CTO - Check this out

CTRN - Can't talk right now

CTS - Change the subject

CU - See you and/or Cracking Up

CU@ - See you around

CU2 - See you, Too

CU2MR - See you tomorrow

CU46 - See You for Sex

CUA - See you around

CUATU - See You around the Universe

CUB - Call you back

CUIAL - See you in another life

CUIMD - See You in My Dreams

CUL - See you later and/or Call You Later and/or Catch You Later

CULA - See you later alligator

CUL8R - See you later

CUL8RM8 - See you later m8

CUMID - See you in my dreams

CUNS - See You in School

CUOL - See You On-line

CURLO - See you around like a donut

CUS - See you soon

CUT - See you tomorrow

CUWTA - Catch Up With the Acronyms

CUZ - Because

CWOT - Complete waste of time

CWYL - Chat with you later

CX – Cancelled

CY - Calm Yourself

CYA – Cover Your Ass and/or See Ya

CYAL8R - See you later

CYB - Call you back

CYDI - Can ya dig it?

CYE - Check your e-mail

CYEP - Close your eyes partner

CYF - Check your Facebook

CYL - See You Later

CYM - Check Your Mail
CYO - See you online
CYR - Call your
CYT - See You Tomorrow
CYWW2BY - See ya, wouldn't want to be ya
cz - Because

"Letter D"
D&M - Deep & Meaningful
D/C - Don't care
d00d - dude, also seen as dood
D2 - Dedos / fingers (Spanish SMS)
D46? - Down for sex?
d8 - Date
da - There
DA - Meaning "The" and/or Dumb Ass
DAC - Duck and Cover
DAE - Dreams are empty
DAH - Dumb ass hole
DAK - Dead at keyboard
DAoC - Dark Age of Camelot
DAMHIKT - Don't Ask Me How I Know That
DAQ - Dumb ass question
DARFC - Ducking and Running for Cover
DAU - Doesn't Add Up
DBA - Doing Business As
DBABAI - Don't Be A Bitch about It
DBAU - Doing business as usual
DBC - Don't Be Cheap
DBD - Don't Be Dumb
DBEYR - Don't believe everything you read
DBG - Don't be gay
DBMN - Don't bug me now
DBS - Dumb Bitch Syndrome and/or Dad behind shoulder
DC – Disconnect

DD - Dear (or Darling) daughter and/or Due Diligence
DDSOS - Different Day, Same Old Sh**
DEGT - Dear (or Darling) daughter
DF - Don't even go there
deets - Details
def – Definitely
DEGT - Don't Even Go There
dem – Them
DENIAL - Don't Even Notice I Am Lying
dese – These
DETI - Don't Even Think It
dewd – dude
dey – they
DF - Dear Friend
DFIK - Darn If I Know
DFL - Dead F***ing last
DFTBA - Don't forget to be awesome
DFU - Don't F*** Up
DGA - Don't go anywhere and/or Digital guardian angel
DGAF - Don't give a F***
DGARA - Don't give a rat's Ass
DGT - Don't go there
DGTG - Don't go there, girlfriend
DGYF - Damn Girl You're Fine
DH - Dear (or Darling) husband and/or Dear Hubby
DHFWM - Don't have fun without me
DHR - Demon Hell Ride
DHU - Dinosaur hugs
DHYB - Don't Hold Your Breath
DIAF - Die in a Fire
DIC - Drunk In Charge
DIIK - Damned If I Know
DIKU - Do I know you?
DILLIGAD - Do I Look Like I Give A Damn
DILLIGAF - Do I look like I give a F***?

DILLIGAFF - Does it look like I give a flying f***?
DILLIGAS - Do I look like I give a sh**?
DINK - Double Incomes, No Kids
DIRFT - Do It Right the First Time
DIS - Did I say?
DISTO - Did I Say That Outloud?
DISTOL - Did I Say That Outloud?
DITG - Down in the gutter
DITYID - Did I tell you I'm distressed?
DITR - Dancing In the Rain
ditto – Same here
DITYID - Did I Tell You I'm Distressed
DIY - Do it yourself
DK - Don't know
DKDC - Don't know, don't care
DKP - Dragon kill points
D/L - Download
DL – Dead Link and/or Down Low and/or Doing Laundry
DLM - Don't leave me
DLO - Down low
DLTBBB - Don't let the bed bugs bite
DLTCU - Don't let them catch you
DLTM - Don't lie to me
DLMBM - Don't let me be misunderstood
DLTBBB - Don't let the bed bugs bite
DLYVM - Don't like you very much
DM - Doesn't matter and/or Direct Message and/or Do Me and/or Dungeon Master
DMI - Don't Mention It
DMNDS - Doesn't make no dang sense
DMNO - Dude Man No Offense
DMY - Don't mess yourself
DN – Down
DNBL8 - Do Not Be Late
DNC - Do not compute (meaning I do not understand)

DND – Do Not Disturb

DNF - Does Not Finish and/or Did Not Finish

DNFTT - Do Not Feed The Trolls

DNPMPL - Damn Near Pissed My Pants Laughing

DNR - Dinner (SMS)

DNT - Don't

DOA - Dead on arrival

DOC - Drug of Choice

DOE - Daughter of Eve and/or Depends On Experience

DOHAB - Dropped on Head at Birth

DOM - Dirty old man

DORD - Department of Redundancy Department

DOS - Dad over shoulder

DOT - Damage over time

DP – Domestic Partner and/or Display Picture

DPS - Damage per second

DPUP - Don't Poop Your Pants

DPWM - Don't play with me

DQ – Dumb Question

DQMOT - Don't quote me on this

DQOTD - Dumb question of the day

DQYDJ - Don't Quit Your Day Job

DR - Didn't read

DRB – Dirty Rat Bastard

DRC - Don't really care

DRIB – Don't Read if Busy

DRK - Don't really know

DRT - Dead Right There

DRTR – Do Right Things Right

DS - Dear (or Darling) son

DSI - Don't sweat it

DSTR8 – Damn Straight

DT - Damn typos

DTC - Deep Throaty Chuckle

DTF - Down to f***

DTR - Define the relationship
DTRT - Do the right thing
DTS - Don't think so
DTTD - Don't touch that dial
DU – Damn You and/or Don't Understand
DUCT - Did you see that?
DUI - Driving Under the Influence
DUK - Didn't you know?
DULM - Do you love me?
DUM - Do You Masturbate?
DUNA - Don't Use No Acronyms
DUPE – Duplicate
dunno – I don't Know
DUR - Do you remember?
DURS - Damn You Are Sexy
DUSL - Do You Scream Loud?
DUST - Did You See That?
DUUT - Do you understand that?
DV8 - Deviate
DW - Dear (or Darling) wife and/or Don't Worry
DWB - Don't Write Back
DWBH - Don't Worry Be Happy
Dweet – Drunken Tweet
DWF - Divorced white female
DWHTGTTA - Do we have to go through this again?
DWI - Driving While Intoxicated
DWIM - Do what I mean
DWIMC - Do What I Mean, Correctly
DWIMNWIS - Do What I Mean, Not What I Say
DWISNWID - Do what I say, not what I do
DWL - Dying with laughter
DWM - Divorced white male
DWPKOTL - Deep Wet Passionate Kiss On the Lips
DWS - Driving While Stupid
DWWWI - Surfing the World Wide Web while intoxicated

DWYM - Does What You Mean
DX - Driving
DXNRY – Dictionary
DYD - Don't you dare?
DYFI - Did you find it?
DYFM - Dude You Fascinate Me
DYHAB - Do You Have A Boyfriend?
DYHAG - Do You Have A Girlfriend?
DYJHIW - Don't you just hate it when...?
DYK - Did you know?
DYLI - Do You Love It?
DYLM - Do you love me? And/or Do you like me?
DYM - Did you mean?
DYNWUTB - Do you know what you are talking about?
DYOFDW - Do Your Own F***ing Dirty Work
DYOR - Do your own research
DYSTSOTT - Did You See the Size of That Thing
DYSWIS - Do you see what I see?
DYTTH - Did you talk to him? And/or Did you talk to her?

"Letter E"
E – Ecstasy and/or Enemy
E1 - Everyone
E123 - Easy as one, two, three
E2EG - Ear to ear grin
E2HO - Each to His/Her Own
ea - Each
EAK - Eating at keyboard
EAPFS - Everything About Pittsburgh F***ing Sucks
EBKAC - Error between keyboard and chair
ECEG – Easy Come Easy Go
ED - Erase display
EE – Electronic Emission
EF4T – Effort
effin - F***ing

EFT - Electronic Funds Transfer

EG - Evil grin and/or For Example

EI - Eat it and/or emotionally intelligent

EIE - Enough is enough

EIP - Editing in progress

EL – Evil Laugh

EM – Excuse Me and/or E-Mail

EMA - E-mail address

EMFBI - Excuse me for butting in

EMFJI - Excuse me for jumping in

EMI - Excuse My Ignorance

EML - Email Me Later

emo - Emotional

EMRTW - Evil Monkey's Rule the World

EMSG - E-mail message

ENUF - Enough

EOD - End of day and/or End of Discussion and/or Explosive Ordinance Disposal

EOF - End of file

EOL - End of lecture and/or End of Life and/or End of Line

EOM - End of message

EOR - End of rant

EOS - End of show

EOT - End of transmission and/or End of Thread

EPIF - Epic Failure

EQ - EverQuest

ERS2 - Eres tz / are you (Spanish SMS)

ES - Erase screen

ESAD - Eat Sh** and die!

ESADFYA - Eat Sh** And Die You F***ing Asshole

ESEMED - Every Second Every Minute Every Day

ESH - Experience, Strength, and Hope

ESMF - Eat Sh** Mother F***er

ESO - Equipment Smarter than Operator

ETA - Estimated time (of) arrival and/or Edited to add

ETD - Estimated time of departure

ETLA - Extended Three Letter Acronym

EVA – Ever

every1 - Everyone

EVO – Evolution

EVRE1 - Every One

EWG - Evil wicked grin (in fun, teasing)

EWI - Emailing while intoxicated

EWO - Eyes Wide Open

EWS - Eyes Wide Shut

EYC - Excitable, yet calm

EZ - Easy

EZY - Easy

"Letter F"

F - Meaning female

F/IB - In the front or in the back

F2F - Face to face

F2P - Free to play

F2T – Free to Talk

F9 - Fine

FAAK - Falling asleep at keyboard

FAB - Features Attributes Benefits

Facepalm - Used to represent the gesture of "smacking your forehead with your palm" to express embarrassment or frustration

FAF - Funny as F***

FAH – F***ing A Hot and/or Funny as Hell

FAP – F***ing A Pissed

FAQ - Frequently asked questions

FAQL - Frequently Asked Questions List

FASB - Fast Ass Son Bitchii

FAWC - For Anyone Who Cares

FAWOFMT - Frequently Argued Waste of My F***ing Time

FAY - F*** All Y'all
FB – F*** Buddy and/or FaceBook
FBF - Fat boy food (e.g. pizza, burgers, fries)
FBFR - FaceBook friend
FBI - F***ing Brilliant Idea and/or Female Body Inspector
FBKS - Failure between Keyboard and Seat
FBM - Fine by me
FBOCD - Facebook Obsessive Compulsive Disorder
FBOW - For better or worse
FBTW - Fine, be that way
FC - Fingers crossed and/or Full Card and/or Future Consideration
FCFS - First Come, First Served
FC'INGO - For Crying Out Loud
FCOL - For Crying Out Loud
FDGB - Fall down Go Boom
FDROTFL - Falling down, rolling on the floor laughing
FE – Fatal Error
FEAR – Forget Everything and Run and/or Face Everything and Recover
FEITCTAJ – F***'em if they can't take a joke
FF - Follow Friday and/or Friends Forever and/or Flying Fadoodle and/or Freeze Frame
FF&PN - Fresh Fields and Pastures New
FFA - Free for all
FFF - Fight for first
FFS - For F*** sakes
FFWE - Finds fault with everything
FGDAI - Fuhgedaboudit and/or Forget About It
FGS - For goodness sake
FH - F***ing Hell and/or Future husband
FICAR - Forget It, Cut and Run
FICCL - Frankly I couldn't care a less
FIF - F*** I'm Funny
FIFO - First In, First Out

FIGMO – F*** It, Got My Orders
FIIK – F*** if I know
FIIOOH - Forget it, I'm out of here
FIL - Father in law
FILF - Father I'd Like to F***
FIMH - Forever in my heart
FINE - F***ed up, Insecure, Neurotic, Emotional
FISH - First in, still here
FITB - Fill in the blank
FLCH - Feels like coming home
FLIE - A flat-out lie
FLUID - F***ing Look it Up, I Did
FML – F*** My Life
FMLTWIA - F*** Me Like the Whore I Am
FMM - Fresh my mind
FMTYEWTK - Far More Than You Ever Wanted To Know
FMUTA - F*** Me Up the Ass
fn – Fine
FNB - Football and beer
FNG - F***ing New Guy
FO - F*** Off and/or Far Out
FOAC - Fall over a cry
FOAD - F*** Off and Die
FOAF - Friend of a Friend
FOAG - F*** Off and Google
FOB - Fell off the Bed and/or Fresh off the Boat
FOC - Free of Charge
FOCL - Falling off the chair laughing
FOFL - Falling on Floor Laughing
FOFLMAO - Falling on the floor laughing my Ass off
FOGC - Fear of Getting Caught
FOL - Fond of Leather
FOMC - Fell off my chair
FOMCL - Falling Off My Chair Laughing
FOOMCL - Falling out of my chair laughing

FOOL - Fresh out of Luck

FOP – F***ing Old People

FORD - Found on road dead

FORGIVE - Faith, Obedience, Righteousness, Grace, Inheritance, Victory, Edify

FOS - Full of Sh** and/or Freedom of Speech and/or Feat of strength and/or Figure of Speech

FOSL - Fear of speed limit

FOTCL - Falling off the chair laughing

FOTD - Face of the day

FOTFL - Falling on the floor laughing

FOTKL - Falling on the keyboard laughing

FOUO - For Official Use Only

FP – Flight Point

FPS - First-person shooter and/or Frames per second

FRED - F***ing Ridiculous Electronic Device

frnd - Friend

FRT - For real though

FS - For Sale

FSBO - For Sale by Owner

FSR - For Some Reason

FSU - F*** Sh** Up

FTASB - Faster Than a Speeding Bullet

FTBOMH - From the bottom of my heart

FTE - Full Time Employee

FTEL - For the epic loss

FTEW - For the epic win

FTF - F*** That's Funny and/or Face To Face

FTFOI - For the Fun of It and/or For the F*** Of It

FTFY - Fixed that for you

FTG - For the group

FTK - For the kill

FTL - For the loss and/or Faster than Light

FTLOG - For the Love of God

FTMFW - For the mother f***ing win

FTMP - For the most part
FTN - F*** That Noise
FTP – Forget the Past
FTR - For the Record
FTRF - F*** That's Really Funny
FTS – F*** That Sh**
FTTB - For the Time Being
FTTT - From time to time
FTW - For the Win and/or F*** the World
FU – F*** you and/or Fully Understood
FU2 - F*** You Too
FUBAR - F***ed Up beyond All Recognition (or Repair)
FUBB - F***ed Up Beyond Belief
FUCT - Failed under continuous testing
FUD - Fear, Uncertainty, and Disinformation/Doubt and/or
Face up Deal
FUJIMO - F*** You Jack I'm Movin' On
FUM - F***ed Up Mess
FURTB - Filled Up and Ready To Burst
FUSIT – F***ed up situation
FUT - Follow up to
FW – Forward and/or Future Wife
FWB - Friend with benefits
FWD - Forward
FWIW - For what it's worth
FWM - Fine with me
FWOT - F***ing Waste of Time
FYA - For Your Amusement
FYE - For Your Edification and/or For your Entertainment
FYEO - For your eyes only
FYF - From Your Friend
FYI - For your information
FYIFV - F*** You I'm Fully Vested
FYL - F*** your life
FYLTGE - From Your Lips to Gods Ears

FYM - For Your Misinformation
FYSBIGTBABN - Fasten Your Seat Belts It's Going To Be A Bumpy Night

"Letter G"
<g> - Grin
G - Guess and/or Grin and/or Giggle
G/F – Girlfriend
G1 - Good One
G2B - Going to bed
G2CU - Good to see you
G2G - Got to go
G2GGS2D - Got to go get something to drink
G2GIAM - Got to go in a minute
G2GICYAL8ER - Got to go I'll see you later
G2GLYS - Got To Go Love Ya So
G2GP - Got to go pee
G2P - Gone to pee
G2PB - Got to pee badly
G2R - Got to run
G2TU - Got to tell u (you)
G4C - Going for coffee
G4I - Go For It
G4N - Good for Nothing
g8r - Great
G9 – Genius and/or Goodnight
GA - Go ahead and/or Good Afternoon
GAB - Getting a Beer
GAC - Get a clue
GAFC - Get a F***ing clue
GAFL - Get A F***ing Life
GAFYK - Get Away From Your Keyboard
GAG - Got any gossip?
GAGA - Go amused, go amazed
GAGFI - Gives a Gay First Impression

GAHOY - Get A Hold of Yourself
GAL - Get a life
GALGAL - Give A Little Get a Little
GALHER - Get A Load of Her
GALHIM - Get A Load of Him
GALMA - Go away, leave me alone
GANB - Getting another Beer
GAP - Got A Pic? And/or Gay Ass People
GAS - Got a second? and/or Greetings and salutations
gawd – God
GAWMA - Go ahead, whet my appetite
GB – Goodbye and/or Good Bridge
GB2W - Get back to work
GBFN - Goodbye for now
GBG - Great Big Grin
GBH - Great Big Hug
GBH&K - Great big hug and kiss
GBHK - Great big hug and kiss
GBR - Garbled beyond recovery
GBTTD - Got better things to do
GBTW - Get back to work
GBU - God bless you
GBY - God bless you
GC - Good Crib and/or Groovy Cat
GD – Good
GD&H - Grinning, ducking, and hiding
GD&R - Grinning, Ducking and Running
GD&RF - Grinning, Ducking and Running Fast
GD&RVF - Grinning, ducking, and running very fast
GD&WVF - Grinning, Ducking, and Walking Very Fast
GDI - God Damn It and/or God Damn Independent
GDW - Grin, Duck and Wave
GE - Good evening
GF - Girl friend
GFETE - Grinning from ear to ear

GFF - Go F***ing Figure
GFFA - Good from Far Away
GFG - Good f***in' game
GFI - Go for it
GFL - Gamer For Life
GFN - Gone For Now and/or Good for Now
GFON - Good for One Night
GFR - Grim File Reaper
GFTD - Gone For the Day
GFU - Good for you
Gfunk - Girlfriend
GFY - Good for You and/or Go F*** Yourself and/or Go Find Yourself
GFYMF - Go F*** Yourself Mother F***er
GG - Good Game and/or Gotta Go and/or Giggling and/or Good Grief
GGA - Good game, all
GGE1 - Good game, everyone
GGG – Giggle and/or Gotta get a grip
GGGB - Good girl gone bad
GGGG - God, God, God, God
GGL - Good game loser
GGMSOT - Gotta get me some of that
GGOH - Gotta Get Outa Here
GGN - Gotta Go Now
GGOGG - Great gobs of goose grease
GGOH - Gotta Get Out of Here
GGP - Got to go pee
GGY - Go Google Yourself
GH - Good hand
GHI - Get Help Immediately
GHM - God Help Me
GI - Google It and/or Good Idea
GIAR - Give it a rest
GIC - Gift in crib and/or God's in Control

40

GICBTS - Gosh, I can't believe that stuff

GICNBY - Gosh, I cannot believe you

GIDK - Gee I Don't Know

GIG - God is good

GIGO - Garbage in, garbage out

GILF - Grandmother I'd like to F***

GIRL - Guy in real life

GIST - Great Ideas for Starting Things

GIT - Get over it

GIWISI - Gee, I wish I said it

GIWIST - Gee, I Wish I'd Said That

GJ - Good job

GJP - Good Job Partner

GK - Go know

GL - Good Luck and/or Get Lost

GL&GH - Good luck and good hunting

GL2U - Good luck to you

GL/HF - Good luck, have fun

GLA - Good luck all

GLB - Good Looking Boy

GLBT - Gay, Lesbian, Bisexual, Transgender - also seen as LBGT

GLE - Good luck everyone

GLE1 - Good luck everyone

GLG - Good Looking Girl

GLGH - Good Luck and Good Hunting

GLHF - Good luck have fun

GLHFTTYL - Good luck, have fun, talk to you later

GLIW - Got lost in web

GLNG - Good luck next game

GLWT - Good luck with that

GLWTN - Guffawing loudly waking up the neighborhood

GLYASDI - God Loves You And So Do I

GM - Good Morning and/or Good Move and/or Good Match

GMAB - Give Me A Break

41

GMAFB - Give ME A F***ing Break
GMBA - Giggling my butt off
GMeSumLuvin - Gimme Some Lovin'
GMTA - Great minds think alike
GMTFT - Great Minds Think for Themselves
GMV - Got my vote
GN - Good night
GNBLFY - Got Nothing but Love for You
GNE1 - Good night everyone
GNIGHT - Good night
GNITE - Good night
GNO - Girls night out
GNOC - Get Naked On Cam
GNSD - Good night, sweet dreams
GNST - Good night, sleep tight
GNU - Good, N' You?
GO - Get Out and/or Get Off
GOG - Gift of god
GOI - Get over it
GOK - God Only Knows
GOL - Giggling out loud and/or groaning out loud
GOLF - Gentlemen only, ladies forbidden
GOMB - Get off my back
GOML - Get on my level
GOOD job - Get out Of Debt job
GOOML - Get out of my life
gonna - Going to
GOS - Gay or Straight
GOTY - Game of the Year
GOWI - Get On With It
GOWM - Go out with me
GOYFA - Get off Your Fat Ass
GOYHH - Get off Your High Horse
GP - Go private
GPOY - Gratuitous picture of yourself

GR - Gotta Run

GR&D - Grinning Running and Ducking

GR2BR - Good Riddance to Bad Rubbish

GR8 – Great

GRAS - Generally Recognized As Safe

GRATZ - Congratulations

GRL – Girl

grrlz - girls, also seen as grrl

GRRR - Growling

GRWG - Get right with God

GrwOldWivMe - Grow Old with Me

GR&D - Grinning, running and ducking

GS - Good shot and/or Good Split

GSC - Gimme Some Credit

GSHIWMP - Giggling so hard I wet my pants

GSOAS - Go Sit On a Snake

GSOH - Good Sense of Humor

GSW - Got some weed

GSYJDWURMNKH - Good Seeing You, Just Don't Wear Your Monkey Hat

GT - Good try

GT2T - Got time to talk

GTBOS - Glad To Be Of Service

GTFO - Get the F*** out and/or Get the F*** off

GTFOOH - Get the F*** Out Of Here

GTG - Got to go and/or Good to Go

GTGB - Got To Go, Bye

GTGP - Got To Go Pee

GTH - Go To Hell

GTK - Good to Know

GTM - Giggle to Myself

GTR - Got to run

GTRM - Going to read mail

GTSY - Great (or good) to see you and/or Glad to see you

GUB - Gross ugly bug and/or gross ugly belly

GUD - Good and/or Geographically UnDesirable
GUFN - Grounded until further notice
GUO - Great Unlucky One
GUTI - Get Used To It
Guvment - government, also seen as guvmint, gumint
gv – Give
gvn – Given
GWHTLC - Glad we had this little chat
GWI - Get with It
GWS - Get Well Soon
GYHOOYA - Get Your Head Out Of Your Ass
GYFO - Get your freak on
GYPO - Get Your Pants Off
GYSR - Gosh, you're so random
gz - Congratulations

"Letter H"
H^ - Hook Up
H – Hug
H&K - Hugs and Kisses
h/o - Hold On
h/p - Hold Please
H2CUS - Hope to see you soon
H2S - Here to Stay
H2SYS - Hope to see you soon
H4U - Hot For You
H4Y – Hot For You
H4XXOR - Hacker and/or To Be Hacked
H8 - Hate
H8TTU - Hate to be you
H9 - Husband in room
HA - Hello again
HABD - Have a blessed day
HABU - Have a better un'
HAC - Have a Cow

44

HADVD - Have Advised
HAG1 - Have a good one
HAGD - Have a Great Day
HAGN - Have A Good Night
HAGO - Have A Good One
HAGS - Have a great summer
HAGW - Have a good week
haha - Laughing
HAK - Hug and kiss
HAN - How about now?
HAND - Have a nice day
HANT - Have a nice time
HAU - How about you?
hav – Have
HAR - Hit and Run
HAWTLW - Hello and Welcome to Last Week
HAY - How are you?
HB - Hurry back and/or Hug back and/or Happy Birthday
HB2U - Happy birthday to you
HBASTD - Hitting Bottom and Starting To Dig
HBB - Hip beyond Belief
H-BDAY - Happy Birthday
HBIB - Hot but Inappropriate Boy
HBIC - Head Bitch in Charge
HBU - How about you?
HC – How Cool
HCC - Holy Computer Crap
HCIT - How cool is that
HD – Hold
HDYLMN - How do you like me now
HDYLTA - How Do You Like Those Apples?
hehe – Laughing
HF - Hello Friend and/or Have Fun and/or Have Faith
HFAC - Holy flipping animal crackers
HFC - Holy f***ing crap

H-FDAY - Happy Father's Day
HFS - Holy F***in S**t!!
HH - Ha-ha and/or Holding Hands
HH1/2KO - Ha-ha, half-kidding only
HHIS - Head hanging in shame
HHJK - Ha-ha, just kidding
HHO1/2K – Ha-Ha, Only Half Kidding
HHOJ - Ha-Ha, Only Joking
HHOK – Ha-Ha, Only Kidding
HHOS - Ha-Ha, Only Serious
HHSF - Ha-ha, so funny
HHTYAY - Happy Holidays to You and Yours
HHVF - Ha-ha, very funny
HI5 - High Five
HidMeClse - Hold Me Close
HIG - How's It Going?
HIH - Hope It Helps
HIOOC - Help, I'm out of Coffee
HITAKS - Hang In There and Keep Smiling
HITULThtILuvU - Have I Told You Lately That I Love You
HIWTH - Hate it when that happens
HJ – Hand Job
HK - Hugs and kisses and/or Hello Kitty
HL - Half Life
HLA - Hola / hello (Spanish SMS)
HLBD - Happy late birthday
HLM - He loves me
H-MDAY - Happy Mother's Day
hm - Home
HMFIC - Head MOFO in Charge
HMS - Hanging myself
HMSL - Holding my sides laughing
HMT - Here's my try
HMU - Hit Me Up
hmwk - Homework

HNL - (w) Hole 'nother level

HNTI - How Nice That/This Is

HNTW - How Nice That Was

HNY - Happy New Year

HO - Hang On and/or Hold On

HOAS - Hold on a second and/or Hell of a Shot

HOF - Hall of fame

HOHA - HOllywood Hacker

HOIC - Hold On, I'm Coming

HOM - Hit or miss

HOPE - Have Only Positive Expectations and/or Highlights of Personal Experience

HORU - How old are you

HOS - Husband over shoulder

HOT - Heal over time

hot-tea - Hottie

HOYEW - Hanging On Your Every Word

HP - Hit points and/or Health points and/or High Power and/or Handphone

HPDC - Happy People Don't Complain

HPOA - Hot Piece of Ass

HPPO - Highest Paid Person in Office

HPS - Heals per second

HRU - How are you?

HSIK - How Should I Know

HSM - High school musical

HT - Hi There and/or Heard Through

HTB - Hang the Bastards

HTC - Hit the cell

HTH - Hope this helps

HTN - High time now

HTNOTH - Hit the Nail on the Head

HTSUS - Hope to see you soon

HU – Hey You and/or Hook Up and/or Hang Up and/or Hold Up

HUA - Heads up Ace and/or Head up Ass
HUB - Head up butt
HUD - How You Doing?
HUGZ – Hugs
huh – what
HUMM - Hope you miss me
HUYA - Head up your Ass
HV - Have
HVH - Heroic Violet Hold (online gaming)
HW – Homework and/or Hardware
HWGA - Here We Go Again
HWP - Height weight proportionate
HWU - Hey, what's up?
HY - Hell yeah
HYL - Help You Later

"Letter I"
I 1-D-R - I Wonder
I%I - Intercourse and inebriation
I <3 U - I Love You
I2 - I too (me too)
I8 – I Ate
I8U - I hate you
i h8 it - i hate it
I&I - Intercourse & Inebriation
I-D-L – Ideal
IA - I agree
IA8 - I already ate
IAAA - I am an accountant
IAAD - I am a doctor
IAAL - I am a lawyer
IAB - In a bit
IAC - In Any Case and/or I Am Confused and/or If Anyone
Cares
IAD - It all depends

IAE - In any event
IAFAIK - As Far As I Know
IAG - It's all good
IAGTKOM - I Ain't Got That Kind of Money
IAGSMSOL - I am getting some money sooner or later
IAGW - In a good way
IAIL - I am in love
IAITS - It's All In the Subject
IAM - In a minute
IANAC - I am not a crook
IANADBIPOOTV - I Am Not A Doctor But I Play One on TV
IANAE - I Am Not an Expert
IANAL - I am not a lawyer
IANNNGC - I Am Not Nurturing the Next Generation of Casualties
IAO - I am out (of here)
IASAP4U - I Always Say a Prayer for You
IAT - I Am Tired and/or Alright
IAW - I Agree With and/or In Accordance With
IAWMP - I almost wet my pants
IAWTC - I agree with the comment
IAYF - It's all your fault
IAYM - I Am Your Master
IB - I'm back
IB2D - I beg to differ
IBGYBG - I'll Be Gone, You'll Be Gone
IBIWISI - I'll Believe It When I See It
IBK - Idiot behind Keyboard
IBRB - I'll Be Right Back
IBT - In Between Technology
IBTC - Itty Bitty Titty Committee
IBTD - I Beg To Differ
IBTL - In Before the Lock
IC - Independent Contractor and/or In Character and/or I See

ICAM - I couldn't agree more

ICBW - It could be worse and/or I could be wrong

ICBWICBM - It Could Be Worse, It Could Be Me

ICCL - I couldn't care less

ICE - In case of emergency

ICEDI - I can't even discuss it

ICFILWU - I could fall in love with you

ICHI - I can't help it

ICL - In Christian Love

ICO - In care of and/or In concern of

ICOCBW - I could, of course, be wrong

ICURNVS - I see you are envious

ICW - I Can't Wait

ICLWYL - I Can't Live Without Your Love

ICYC - In Case You're Curious and/or In Case You Care

ICYMI - In case you missed it (Twitter slang)

ID10T - Idiot

IDBI - I don't believe it

IDC - I don't care

IDEK - I don't even know

IDFK - I don't f***ing know

IDGAD - I Don't Give a Damn

IDGAF - I don't give a F***

IDGARA - I Don't Give a Rats Ass

IDGI - I Don't Get It and/or I Don't Get Involved

IDGRA - I don't give a rat's ass

IDHI - I don't have it

IDI - I doubt it

IDK - I don't know

IDKTMWIM - I Don't Know Tell Me What It Means

IDKY - I don't know you and/or I don't know why

IDM - It Does Not Matter

IDMB - I'll do my best

IDN - I don't know

IDNDT - I did not do that

IDNK - I do not know
IDR - I don't remember
IDRK – I Don't Really Know
IDS - I'm dead serious
IDST - I Didn't Say That
IDT - I don't think
IDTA - I Did That Already
IDTS - I don't think so
IDTT - I'll drink to that
IDU - I don't understand
IDUNNO - I don't know
IE - That is
IF/IB - In the Front and/or In the Back
IFAB - I Found a Bug
IFF - If and only if
IFLY - I f***ing love you
IFOCN - In front of computer naked
IFSFY - I feel sorry for you
IFU - I F***ed Up
IFVB - I feel very bad
IFYP - I feel your pain
IG - I guess
IG2P - I got to pee
IG2R - I got to run
IGGP - I Gotta Go Pee
iggy - Ignored
IGHT - I got high tonight
IGI - I get it
IGN - I (I've) got nothing
IGP - I gotta pee
IGTP - I Get the Point and/or I got to pee
IGWS - It Goes Without Saying
IGWST - It Goes Without Saying That
IGYHTBT - I Guess You Had To Be There
IH8U - I hate you

IHA - I Hate Acronyms
IHAIM - I Have another Instant Message
IHI – I hate it
IHNI - I have no idea
IHNO - I Have No Opinion
IHTFP - I Have Truly Found Paradise and/or I Hate This F***ing Place
IHU - I hear you and/or I hate you
IHY - I hate you
II - I'm impressed
IIABDFI - If It Ain't Broke, Don't Fix It
IIIO - Intel inside, idiot outside
IIMAD - If It Makes an(y) Difference
IINM - If I'm Not Mistaken
IIOK - If I only knew
IIR - If I Remember and/or If I Recall
IIRC - If I Remember Correctly and/or If I Recall Correctly
IIT - Is It Tight? And/or I'm impressed too
IITLYTO - If it's Too Loud You're Too Old
IITM - It's In the Mail
IITRT - it is the right time
IITYWIMWYBMAD - If I Tell You What It Means Will You Buy Me a Drink
IITYWYBMAD - If I Tell You Will You Buy Me a Drink
IIWM - If It Were Me
IJC2SILU - I just called to say I love you
IJDGAF - I just don't give a f***
IJPMP - I Just Pissed My Pants
IJS - I'm just saying...
IJWTK - I Just Want To Know
IJWTS - I Just Want To Say
IK - I know
IKALOPLT - I Know A Lot of People Like That
IKHYF - I know how you feel
IKR - I know, right?

IKU - I kill you
IKWUM - I know what you mean
IKWYM - I Know What You Mean
IKYABWAI - I Know You Are But What Am I?
IKYD - I know you did
ILBL8 - I'll be late
ILA - I Love Acronyms
ILAMY - I love and miss you
ILF/MD - I Love Female/Male Dominance
ILICISCOMK - I Laughed, I Cried, I Spat/Spilt
Coffee/Crumbs/Coke on My Keyboard
ILMJ - I Love My Job
ILMM - I love my man
ILU - I love you and/or I like You
ILUAAF - I Love You as A Friend
ILUB - I love you baby
ILUGTD - I love you guys to death
ILUM - I love you man
ILUVU - I love you
ILY - I love you
ILY2 - I love you too
ILYFAE - I love you forever and ever
ILYFE - I love you for eternity
ILYK - I'll let you know
ILYL - I love you lots
ILYLC - I love you like crazy
ILYMTYWEK - I love you more than you would ever know
ILYSM - I love you so much
ILYWAMH - I love you with all my heart
IM - Instant message
IM2BZ2P - I aM Too Busy to (even) Pee
IMA – I might add and/or I'm
IMAO - In my arrogant opinion
IMCO - In My Considered Opinion
IMD - In my dreams

IME – In might experience
IMEZRU - I Am Easy, Are You?
IMF - International Mother Fund
IMGC - I Might Get Caught
IMHARO - In my humble and respectful opinion
IMHBMAO - In my humble but most accurate opinion
IMHEIUO - In My High Exalted Informed Unassailable Opinion
IMHO - In my humble opinion and/or In my honest opinion
IMIO - In my infallible opinion
IMJS - I'M Just Saying
ImL - Means I love you (a way of using the American Sign Language in text)
imma - I'm gonna
IMN2U - I'm Into You
IMNERHO - In My Never Even Remotely Humble Opinion
IMNSHO - In my not so humble opinion
IMNSVHO - In my not so very humble opinion
IMNT - I am not!
IMO - In my opinion
IMOBO - In my own biased opinion
IMOO - In My Own Opinion
IMOT - I'm on that
IMPOV - In My Point Of View
IMR - I Mean Really
IMRU - I Am, Are You
IMS - I am sorry and/or In a Manner of Speaking and/or If memory serves
IMSB - I am so bored
IMSO - In my sovereign opinion
ImT14U - I'm The One for You
imtg - In meeting
IMTM - I am the man
IMU - I miss u (you)
IMVHU - In my very humble opinion

IMVU - Instant Messaging Virtual Universe
IMY - I miss you
IMYA - I miss you already
INAL - I'm not a lawyer
INBD - It's No Big Deal
INC - Meaning "incoming"
INMP - It's Not My Problem
INNW - If Not Now, When
INPO - In No Particular Order
INR - I know right
INRS - It's not rocket science
INT - Is not
INU - I need you
INUCOSM - It's No Use Crying Over Spilt Milk
inv - Invite
IOH - I'm Outta Here
IOHE4U - I Only Have Eyes for You
IOIT - I'm on Irish time
IOMH - In over my head
ION - Index of Names
IONO - I Don't Know
IOT - In Order To
IOU - I Owe You
IOU1 - I owe you 1
IOUD - Inside, Outside, Upside Down
IOW - In other words
IOWAN2BWU - Only Want to Be With You
IPN - I'm Posting Naked
IPO - Initial public offering
IR – In Room
IR8 - Irate
IRDK - I really don't know
IRL - In real life
IRMC - I rest my case
IRSTBO - It really sucks the big one

IRT - In regards to
IS - I'm sorry
ISAGN - I See A Great Need
ISH - Insert Sarcasm Here and/or I'm so hungry and/or Issues
ISLY - I still love you
ISO - In Search Of and/or Is seeking other
ISS - I said so and/or I'm So Sure
ISSYGTI - I'm So Sure You Get the Idea
ISTICSF - I'm So Tired I Could Sleep Forever
ISTM - It Seems To Me
ISTR - I Seem To Remember
ISWC - If Stupid Were a Crime
ISWYM - I See What You Mean
ISYALS - I'll Send You a Letter Soon
ITA - I Totally Agree
ITAM - It's The Accounting, Man (financial blogs)
ITBOOTP - In the bathroom, out of toilet paper
ITFA - In the Final Analysis
ITIGBS - I Think I'm Going to Be Sick
ITILY - I think I like you and/or I think I love you
ITM - In the Money
ITMA - It's That Man Again
ITMT - In the meantime
ITRW - In the real world
ITS - Intense Text Sex
ITSFWI - If the Shoe Fits Wear It
ITTWACW - I thought this was a Christian website
ITYF - I think you'll find
ITYK - I thought you knew
ITYM - I think you're mean
ITYS - I told you so
IUM - If You Must
IUSS - If you say so
IVL - In virtual life
IW2BWU - I want to be with you

IWALU - I will always love you
IWALY - I will always love you
IWAWO - I want a way out
IWBAPTAKYAIYSTA - I Will Buy a Plane Ticket and Kick Your Ass If You Say That Again
IWBNI - It Would Be Nice If
IWFU - I Wanna F*** You
IWIAM - Idiot wrapped in a moron
IWIWU - I Wish I Was You
IWSN - I Want Sex Now
IWTAAQ - I Want to Ask a Question
IWTY - I would tickle you
IWU - I want you
IYAOYAS - If You Ain't Ordinance You Ain't Sh**
IYD - In Your Dreams
IYDMMA - If You Don't Mind My Asking
IYFD - In Your F***ing Dreams
IYFEG - Insert Your Favorite Ethnic Group
IYKWIM - If you know what I mean
IYKWAMAITYD - If You Know What I Mean and I Think You Do
IYO - In your opinion
IYQ - Meaning "I like you"
IYSS - If you say so
IYSWIM - If You See What I Mean

"Letter J"
j00 - You
j00r – Your
J - Joking
J2LYK - Just To Let You Know
J4F - Just For Fun
J4G - Just For Grins
J4I - Just for information
J4T and/or JFT - Just For Today

J5M - Just Five Minutes

JAC - Just a second

JAD - Just Another day

JAFM – Just a F***ing Minute

JAFO - Just Another F***ing Onlooker

JAFS - Just a F***ing Salesman

JAM - Just a minute

JAS - Just a second

JASE - Just another system error

JBC - Just because

JBUG - Just Between Us Girls

JC (J/C) - Just checking and/or Just Curious and/or Just Chilling and/or Jesus Christ

JCR - Jenny Craig Reject

JDI - Just do it

JDMJ - Just Doing My Job

JEOMK - Just Ejaculated On My Keyboard

JFF - Just for fun

JFGI - Just F***ing Google it

JFH - Just F*** Her

JFI - Just For Information

JFK - Just f***ing kidding

JHO - Just Helping Out

JHOMF - Just Helping Out My Friend(s)

JIC - Just in case

JJ (J/J) - Just joking

JJA - Just joking around

JJYW - Just joking with you

JK (J/K) - Just kidding

JLMK - Just let me know

JM2C - Just My 2 Cents

JMHO - Just my humble opinion

JMO - Just my opinion

J/O – Jerking Off

JOOC - Just out of curiosity

JOOTT - Just One of Those Things
JP - Just playing
JS - Just saying
JSU - Just Shut Up
JSYK - Just So You Know
JT (J/T) - Just teasing
JTLYK - Just to let you know
JUADLAM - Jumping Up And Down Like a Monkey
JUIL - Just you I love
JV - Meaning "joint venture"
JW - Just wondering

"Letter K"
K4U and/or K4Y - Kiss for you
K8T - Katie
K – Okay and/or Kiss
kas - Kicking and screaming
KB - Kick Butt and/or Kiss Back
KBD – Keyboard
KC - Keep cool
KDFU - Means Cracking (K) the (D as in Da) F***ing up
kewl – it means cool
KEYA - I will key you later
KEYME - Key me when you get in
KFY - Kiss for You
KHYF - Know How You Feel
KIA - Killed In Action
KIAP - Know It All Pain
KIBO - Knowledge In, Bullsh** Out
KIPPERS - Kids in Parents' Pockets Eroding Retirement Savings
KIR - Keep It Real
KISS - Keep it simple, stupid
KIT - Keep in touch
KITTY – Meaning Vagina

KK - Kiss Kiss and/or Knock, knock and/or Okay, Okay!

KKWT - Knock knock, who's there?

kl - Cool

KM – Kiss Me

KMA - Kiss my Ass

KMAB - Kiss my ass bitch

KMB - Kiss my butt

KMBA - Kiss My Black Ass

KMFHA - Kiss My Fat Hairy Ass

KMIA – Kiss my Italian Ass

KMK - Kiss my keister

KMMFA – Kiss my mother f***ing ass

KMP - Keep Me Posted

KMRIA - Kiss My Royal Irish Arse

KMS - Killing me softly

KMSL - Killing Myself Laughing

KMSLA - Kiss My Shiny Little Ass

KMSO - Knocked my socks off

KMT - Kiss my tushie

KMUF - Kiss Me You Fool

KMWA - Kiss My White Ass

KNIM - Know what I mean?

KNOW - Meaning "knowledge"

KOC - Kiss on cheek

KOK - Knock

KOL - Kiss on lips

KOS - Kid over shoulder and/or Kill on site

KOTC - Kiss on the Cheek

KOTL - Kiss on the lips

KOW - Knock on wood

KPC - Keeping parents clueless

KPTONDL - Keep it on the down low

KS - Kill Stealer

KSC - Kind (of) sort (of) chuckle

KT – Katie

kthx - OK, Thanks
kthxbi - OK thanks, bye
KUTGW - Keep up the good work
kw - Know
KWIM - Know What I Mean?
KWIS - Know what I'm saying
kwl - Cool
KWSTA - Kiss with Serious Tongue Action
KYBC - Keep Your Bum Clean
KYFC - Keep Your Fingers Crossed
KYNC - Keep Your Nose Clean
KYPO - Keep Your Pants On
KYSOTI - Keep Your Stick on the Ice

"Letter L"
L?^ - Let's hook up
L/F/E/ - Lovers forever
L2G - Like to go? And/or Love To Go
L2K - Like to come
L2P - Learn to play
l33t - Leet, meaning 'elite'
L7 – Square
L8 - Late
L8R - Later
L8RG8R - Later, gator
L – Laughing
LA - Laughing a lot
LABATYD - Life's a Bitch and Then You Die
laf – Laugh
laffing – Laughing
LAFS - Love at first sight
LAGNAF - Lets All Get Naked and F***
LAL - Laugh a little and/or laughing a lot
LAM - Leave a message
LAQ - Lame Ass Quote

61

LAST - Locate, Access, Stabilize, Transport
LAWKI - Life As We Know It
lawl - LOL
LB?W/C - Like Bondage? Whips or Chains
LBAY - Laughing back at you
LBD - Lesbian by Default
LBF - Later, best friend
LBM - Little Bitch Man
LBR - Little Boy's Room
LBUG and LBIG - Laughing because you're Gay and/or Laughing Because I'm Gay
LC - Let's celebrate
LD - Long Distance and/or Later Dude
LDIMEDILLIGAF - Look Deeply Into My Eyes, Does It Look Like I Give A F***
LDO - Like, duh obviously
LDR - Long Distance Relationship
LDTTWA - Let's Do the Time Warp Again
LEMENO - Let me know
LEP - Love emo people
LERK - Leaving easy reach of keyboard
LF - Let's F*** and/or Looking For
LF1M - Looking for one more
LFD - Left for day
LFG - Looking for group and/or looking for guard
LFK - Let's French kiss
LFM - Looking for more
LFTD - Laugh for the day and/or Left for the day
LFTI - Looking Forward To It
LFW - Looking for work
LG - Lovely greetings
LGH - Let's get high
LGMAS - Lord Give Me a Sign
LGR - Little Girl's Room
LH6 - Let's have sex

LHSX - Let's have sex
LHM - Lord help me
LHO - Laughing head off
LHOS - Lets Have Online Sex
LHSO - Let's Have Sex Online
LHU - Let's Hook Up and/or Lord Help Us
LHUA - Lord help us all
LI – LinkedIn
LIB - Lying In Bed
LIC - Like I care
LIFO - Last In, First Out
LIG – Life Is Good
LIK – Meaning liquor
lil - Little
LIMT - Laugh in my tummy
LIQ - Laughing inside quietly
LIS - Laughing In Silence
LJBF - Let's Just Be Friends
LKITR - Little Kid in the Room
LL - Later loser
LL&P and/or LLAP - Live Long and Prosper!
LLC - Laughing like crazy
LLGB - Love, later, God bless
LLOL - Literally laughing out loud
LLOM - Like Leno on Meth
LLPOF - Liar liar pants on fire
LLS - Laughing like *silly*
LLT - Looks like Trouble
LLTA - Lots and Lots of Thunderous Applause
LM – Letter Mailed
LM4A~##*zzzz*> - Let's Meet For A Joint
LMA - Leave me alone
LMAO - Laughing my ass off
LMAOROF - Laughing my ass off rolling on the floor
LMAOROTF - Laughing my ass off and rolling on the floor

LMAOTC - Laughing my ass off the chair
LMBO - Laughing my butt off
LMBAO - Laughing My Black Ass Off
LMFAO - Laughing my F***ing Ass off and/or Laughing my fat ass off
LMFAOPIMP - Laughing my freaking ass off peeing in my pants
LMFBO - Laughing my fat butt off
LMGTFY - Let me Google that for you
LMHO - Laughing My Head Off and/or Laughing my hiney off
LMIRL - Lets meet in real life
LMK - Let me know
LMKHTWOFY - Let Me Know How That Works Out For You
LMMFAO - Laughing my mother F***ing Ass off
LMNK - Leave my name out
LMO - Let's make out and/or Leave me one
LMOA - Left a Message On your Answering machine
LMS - Let Me See
LMSO - Laughing My Socks Off
LMTC - Left a Message to Contact
LMTCB - Left Message to Call Back
LMWAO - Laughing my white ass off
LNK – Love and kisses
LNT – Meaning lost in translation
LOA – List of acronyms
LOB – Lying On Bed
LOC – Load of Crap
LOE – Level of Effort
LOFL – Laughing out f***in' loud
LOI – Laughing on the inside
LOL – Laughing Out Loud and/or Lots of Love and/or Lots of Luck and/or Little Old Lady

LOLA – Laugh Out Loud Again and/or Love often, laugh a lot

LOLAWS – Laugh out loud and with style

LOLH – Laughing out loud hysterically

LOLHK – Lots of love, hugs, and kisses

LOLO – Lots of love

LOLOL - Lots of laugh out louds

LOLROFLMAO - Laughing out loud, rolling on floor, laughing my ass off

LOLUSA - Laughing out loud until sides ache

LOLV - Lots Of LoVe

LOLWTF - Laughing out loud (saying) "What the F***?"

LOLZ - Lots of Laughs

LOM - Laugh out Major

LOMBARD - Lots Of Money but a Real Dick

LOML - Love of My Life

LOMLILY - Light of my life, I love you

LONH - Lights On, Nobody Home

LOOL - Laughing Outrageously Out Loud

LOQ - Laugh out quietly

LOPSOD - Long On Promises, Short on Delivery

LORE - Learn Once, Repeat Everywhere

LOS – Line of Site

LOTFLOL - Lying on the floor laughing out loud

LOTI - Laughing on the inside

LOTR - Lord of The Rings

LOU - Laughing Over You

LOVE - Lots of Voluntary Effort and/or Lusting Over Virtually Everyone

LPC - Lead Pipe Cinch

LPOS - Lazy Piece Of Sh**

LQL - Laughing Quite Loudly

LQTM - Laughing quietly to myself

LRF - Little Rubber Feet

LRL - Laugh real loud

LRU - Least Recently Used

LSHIFOMD - Laughing so hard I fell off my dinosaur

LSHITIPAL - Laughing So Hard I Think I Peed A Little

LSHMBH - Laugh so hard my belly hurts

LSHMBIB - Laughing so hard my belly is bouncing

LSHMSFOAIDMT - Laughing so hard my sombrero fell off and I dropped my taco

LSS - Long story short

LST - Long-sleeve t-shirt

LSV - Language, sex and violence

LTD - Living the dream and/or Lovers till death

LTHTT - Laughing Too Hard To Type

LTIC - Laughing 'Til I Cry

LTIO - Laughing Til I Orgasm

LTLWDLS - Let's twist like we did last summer

LTM - Laughing To Myself

LTMQ - Laughing to myself quietly

LTNS - Long time no see

LTNT - Long Time, No Type

LTOD - Laptop of death

LTP - Let's talk privately

LTR - Long Term Relationship and/or Letter and/or Later

LTS - Laughing to self

LtsGt2gthr - Let's Get Together

LTTIC - Look the Teacher Is Coming

LU - Love you

lu4ever - Love your forever

LUA - Love you a lot

LUB - Love you, bye

LUGLS - Love you guys like sisters

LUL - Love you lots

LULAB - Love you like a brother

LULAF - Love you like a friend

LULAS - Love you like a sister

LULU - Locally Undesirable Land Use

LULT - Love you long time
LULZ - Slang for LOL
LUM - Love you man
LUMTP - Love You More Than Pie
LUSM - Love You So Much
LUTA - Let us talking again
luv - Love
Luv2LuvUBab - Love To Love You Baby
LUWAMH - Love You with All My Heart
luzr – Loser
lv - Love
LV1 - Leave one
lvl - Level
LVM - Left voice mail
LWOS - Laughing without smiling
LWR - Launch When Ready
LWT - Laughing with tears
LY - Love ya and/or Love You
LY4E - Love You Forever
LYA - Love You All and/or Love You Always
LYB - Love You Babe
LYCYLBB - Love You, See You Later, Bye Bye
LYK - Let you know
LYKYAMY - Love You, Kiss You, Already Miss You
LYL - Love You Lots
LYLAB - Love You Like a Brother
LYLAS - Love you like a sister
LYLC - Love you like crazy
LYMI - Love You, Mean It
LYMY - Love You Miss You
lyn - Lying
LYSM - Love you so much
LYWAMH - Love You with All My Heart

"Letter M"
m - Male
M$ - Microsoft
M$ULkeCrZ - Miss You Like Crazy!
M.02 - My two cents
M/F - Male or female
M02 - My two cents
M2NY - Me Too, Not Yet
M4C - Meet for Coffee
m4w - men for women
M8 and/or M8s – Mate and/or Mates
MA - Mature Audience
mab – Maybe
mats - Materials
MAYA - Most Advanced Yet Accessible
MB - Mamma's boy and/or Message Board and/or My Bad
MBA - Married But Available
MBF - My best friend
MBN - Must Be Nice
MBRFN - Must Be Real F***ing Nice
MBS - Mom behind shoulder
MC - Merry Christmas
MCAAHNY - Merry Christmas and a happy new year
MCIBTY - My computer is better than yours
MD - Doctor of Medicine and/or Managing Director
MD@U - Mad at you
MD@UFN - Mad at you for now
MDIAC - My Dad is a cop
MDPS - Melee damage per second
MDR - Mort De Rire
me2 - Me too
MEGO - My eyes glaze over
meh - Whatever
MEH - Meaning a "shrug" or shrugging shoulders and/or
Meaning a "so-so" or "just okay"

MEHH - Meaning a "sigh" or sighing
MEZ - Meaning "mesmerize"
MF - My Friend and/or Mother F***er
MFB - Mother F***ing Bitch
MFD - Multi-Function Device
MfG - Mit freundlichen Gruessen
MFI - Mad for it
MFIC - Mother F***er In Charge
MFWIC - Mo Fo Who's In Charge
MG - Many greetings
MGB - May God bless
MGMT – Management
MHBFY - My Heart Bleeds For You
mhhm - uh huh and/or yeah
mhm - Mm-hmm
MHOTY - My Hat's Off To You
MIA - Missing In Action
MIB - Men in Black
MIBG - Mental image be gone
MIH - Make It Happen
MIHAP - May I Have Your Attention Please
MIL - Mother-In-Law
MILF - Mother I'd Like to F***
MAMAS - May I make a suggestion
min – Minute
mins – Minutes
MIPS - Millions of Instructions per Second
MIRL - Meet in real life
mishu - Miss you
MITIN - More Info Than I Needed
mk – Okay
MKA - Make additions
MKAY - Meaning "Mmm, okay"
MKOP - My Kind of Place
MLA - Multiple Letter Acronyms

MLIA - My life is average
MLM - Meaning give the middle finger
MLAS - My Lips Are Sealed
mlm - giving the digital middle finger
MM – Market Maker and/or Missing My and/or Merry Meet and/or Make Me and/or Music Monday
MMA – Meet Me AT
MMAMP - Meet me at my place
MMB - Message me back
MMFU - My mate fancies you
MMHA2U - My Most Humble Apologies to You
MMHRD - Many Many Happy Returns of the Day
MMK - Meaning okay?
MML - Made Me Laugh
MMOB - Mind my own business
MMRD - My mind is rolled down
MMYT - Mail Me Your Thoughts
MNC - Mother Nature calls
mng – Manage
mngr – Manager
MNSG - Mensaje (message in Spanish)
MorF - Male or female?
MO - Move On
mob - Mobile
MOF - Matter of Fact
MOFO - Mother F***er
MOH - Maid of Honor and/or Medal of Honor
MOMBOY - Mamma's boy
MOMPL - One Moment Please
MOO - Mud, Object-Oriented and/or Matter of Opinion and/or My own Opinion
MOOS - Member of the opposite sex
MOP - MOment Please
MOR - Middle of the road
MorF - Male or Female

MOS - Mother over shoulder
MOSS - Member of same sex
MOTAS - Member of the Appropriate Sex
MOTD - Message of the Day
MOTOS - Member(s) Of the Opposite Sex
MOTSS - Member(s) Of the Same Sex
MOTU - Masters of the Universe
MP - Mana points and/or Merry Points
MPFB - My Personal F*** Buddy
MR - Mentally Retarded
MRA - Moving Right Along
MRPH - Mail the Right Place for Help
MRT - Modified ReTweet
MRU - Most recently used
Ms - Miss
MSB - My sexy Bitch
MSG - Message
MSMD - Monkey See Monkey Do
MSN - Moronic Satanic Network
MSNUW - Mini-Skirt No UnderWear
MST - Must see today
MSTM - Makes Sense to Me
MT - Mistype
MTBF - Mean Time before Failure
MTE – My Thoughts Exactly
MTF - More to follow
MTFBWU - May the force be with you
MTFBWY - May the Force Be With You
mtg - Meeting
mth – Month
MTLA - My True Love Always
MTSBWY - May the Schwartz Be With You
MU - Miss U (you)
MU@ - Meet you at
MUAH - Multiple unsuccessful attempts (at/to) humor

MUBAR - Messed up Beyond All Recognition
MUSL - Missing You Sh** Loads
MUSM - Miss you so much
MVA - Motor Vehicle Accident
MVA no PI - Motor Vehicle Accident with no Personal Injury
MVA w/PI - Motor Vehicle Accident with Personal Injury
MW - Most welcome
MWA - Kiss
MWAH - Meaning "kiss" (it is the sound made when kissing through the air)
MWBRL - More Will Be Revealed Later
MYB - myYearbook
MYL – Mind Your Language
MYO - Mind your own (business)
MYOB - Mind your own business

"Letter N"
n – And and/or In
n00b – Newbie
N – No
N-A-Y-L - In a While
N/A - Not Applicable and/or Not Affiliated and/or Not Available
N/C – Not Cool
n00b - Newbie
N1 - Nice one
N1C - No one cares
N2M - Nothing too much
N2MJCHBU - Not Too Much Just Chillin, How Bout You
N2W - Not to worry
N4E - Never forever
n8kd - Naked
NA – No Access
NAB - Not a Blonde

NAC - Not a Clue and/or Not a Chance
NADT - Not a damn thing
NAGB - Nearly Almost a Good Bridge
NAK - Nursing At Keyboard
Nal - Nationality
NALOPKT - Not a lot of people know that
NANA - Not now, no need
NASCAR - Non-Athletic Sport Centered Around Rednecks
natch – Naturally
NATO - No Action, Talk Only
NAVY - Never Again Volunteer Yourself
NAZ - Name, Address, Zip (also means Nasdaq)
NB - Nota Bene and/or Not Bad and/or Please Note
NB4T - Not Before Time
NBA - Nice Big Ass
NBC - Nobody Cares
NBD - No big deal
NBFAB - No bad for a beginner
NBFABS - Not Bad For A Bot Stopper
NBG - No Bloody Good
NBIF - No Basis in Fact
NBJF - No brag, just fact
NBL - Not bloody likely
NBLFY - Nothing but Love for You
NBS - No Bull Sh**
NBSP - No bull s*** please
NC - Nice crib and/or No Comment and/or Not Cool and/or Nice Call
NCG - New College Graduate
NCZ - No capture zone
ND - Nice double and/or No Date and/or and
NDN - Indian
ne – Any
ne-ways - Anyways
NE1 – Anyone

ne14kfc – Anyone for KFC

ne1er – Anyone Here?

Ne2H - Need to Have

NEET - Not currently Engaged in Employment, Education, or Training

nemore – Anymore

NERFAR - Not Emotionally Ready For A Relationship

NES - Never ending story

NESEC - Any Second

nethng - Anything

NEV – Neighborhood Electric Vehicle

neway - Anyway

NEWS - North, East, West, South

NFBSK - Not For British School Kids

NFC - Not Favorably Considered and/or No F***ing Chance

NFE - No F***ing Excuses

NFF - No F***ing Fair

NFG - Not F***ing Good

NFI - No F***ing Idea and/or No further information

NFL - Not F***in' likely

NFM - None for me / not for me

NFS - Need for Sex and/or Network File System and/or Need for Speed and/or Not for sale

NFW - No F***ing Way and/or No Feasible Way and/or Not for Work

NFWS - Not for work safe

NG – No Good

NGE - Not good enough and/or never good enough

NH - Nice hand

NHOH - Never Heard Of Him/Her

NI4NI - An Eye for Any Eye

NIB - New in box

NICE - Nonsense in Crappy Existence

NIFOC - Naked in front of computer

NiCMO - Non-Committal Making Out

NIGI - Now I get it
NIGYYSOB - Now I've Got You, You Son of a B*tch
NIH - Not Invented Here
NIM - No Internal Message
NIMBY - Not in my back yard
NIMJD - Not In My Job Description
NIMQ - Not In My Queue
NIMY - Never In A Million Years
NINO - Nothing In, Nothing Out and/or No Input, No Output
NIROK - Not in reach of keyboard
NISM - Need I Say More
NITL - Not In This Lifetime
NIYFWD - Not in Your Wildest F***ing Dreams
NJ – No Joke and/or Nice Joke
NK - No kidding
NKZ - No kill zone
NL - Not likely
NLL - Nice Little Lady
NLT - No later than
NM - Nothing much and/or Never Mind and/or Nice Meld
nm, u - not much, you?
NME - Enemy
NMH - Not much here
NMHJC - Not much here, just chilling
NMJC - Nothing much, just chilling
NMJCY - Not much, just chilling, you?
NMP - Not My Problem
NMTE - Now More than Ever
NMTN - Nevermind that now
NMU - Not much, you?
NN - Not Now and/or Need and/or Nothing New
NN2R - No need to reply
NNCIMINTFZ - Not Now Chief, I'm In the F ***in' Zone
NNITO - Not necessarily in that order
NNM - Nodding Neck Movement

NNR - Need Not Respond
NNTO - No need to open
NNTR - No need to reply
NNWW - Nudge, Nudge, Wink, Wink
NO - Not Online and/or Know
no praw - no problem
NO1 - No one
NOA - Not Online Anymore
NOBMR - None of my business, right
NOFI - No OFfence Intended
NOFL - No Other Form(s) Listed
NOIRL - No one is really laughing
NOM - No offense meant
NOMB - None of my business
NOOB - Meaning someone who is bad
NORF - No Observable Redeeming Features
NOS - New Old Stock
NOTD - Nail of the day
NOTTOMH - Not off the top of my head
NOW - No way out
NOWL - Meaning "knowledge"
NOY - Not Online Yet
NOYB - None of your business
NP - No problem and/or Neopets
NPC - Non-playing character
NPS - No problem sweetie and/or Net Positive Suction
NQA - No Questions Asked
NQOCD - Not Quite Our Class Dear
NQT - Newly qualified teacher
NR - Nice roll
NRG - Energy
NRN - No response/reply necessary and/or Not Right Now
NS - Nice score and/or Nice Set and/or Nice Split and/or No Sh**
NSA - No strings attached

NSFW - Not safe for work and/or Not suitable for women

NSFS - Not Safe For School

NSISR - Not sure if spelled right

NSN - Never say never

NSS - No S*** Sherlock

NSTLC - Need Some Tender Loving Care

NT - Nice try and/or No Text and/or No Trust and/or No Thanks

NTA - Not This Again

NTBN - No Text Back Needed

NTHING - Nothing (SMS)

NTIM - Not That It Matters

NTL - Never too late

NTMY - Nice to meet you

NTN - No thanks needed

NITMM - Not That It Matters Much

NTK - Nice To Know

NTM - Not That Much

NTMU - Nice To Meet You

NTS - Note to self

NTTAWWT - Not That There's Anything Wrong With That

NTW - Not To Worry

NTY - No thank you

NTYMI - Now That You Mention It

NU – Need You

NUB - New person to a site or game

NUFF - Enough Said

nufn – Nothing

NUIGB - Not until I get back

NVM - Never mind

NVNG - Nothing Ventured, Nothing Gained

NVR – Never

NVRM - Never mind

NW - No way

NWAL - Nerd without a Life

NWO – No Way Out
NWOT - New WithOut Tags
NWR - Not Work Related
NWT - New With Tags
nxt - Next
NYB – Not Your Business
NYC - Not Your Concern
NYCFS - New York City Finger Salute

"Letter O"
O&O - Over and out
O4U - Only for you
O - Opponent and/or Over and/or Meaning "hugs"
OA - Online auctions and/or Over Acting
OAO - Over And Out
OAR - On a roll
OATUS - On a totally unrelated subject
OAUS - On an Unrelated Subject
OB - Oh baby and/or Oh Brother and/or Obligatory and/or Office Bitch
OBE - Overcome By Events
OBO - Or Best Offer
OBTW - Oh By The Way
OBX - Old Battle Axe
OC - Original Character and/or Own Character and/or Of Course
OCD - Obsessive Compulsive Disorder
OD - Over Doing It
ODTAA - One Damn Thing after Another
OE - Operator error
OEM - Original Equipment Manufacturer
ofc - of course
OFL - Out for lunch
OG - Original gangster
OH – Overheard

ohemgee - Oh my gosh
OI - Operator indisposed
OIB - Oh, I'm back
OIC - Oh, I see
OICN - Oh, I see now
OICU812 - Oh I See, You Ate One Too
OJ - Only joking
OK – One Kiss and/or All Correct
OL - Old lady
OLL - Online love
OLN - OnLine Netiquette
OLO - Only Laughed Once
OLPC - One Laptop per Child
OLTL - One Life to Live
OM - Old man and/or Oh, my and/or Oh, Man
OMAA - Oh, my aching Ass (butt)
OMB - Oh My Buddha
OMCD - Old Married Couple Disorder
OMD - Oh my darn!
OMDB - Over my dead body
OMFG - Oh my F***ing God
Omfglmaobbqroflcopteriss - oh my F***ing god, laugh my ass off, owned, roll on floor spinning around I'm so sad
OMFGYASB – Oh my f***ing God, you're a sexy beast
OMG - Oh my God
OMGD - Oh my God, duh
OMGF - Oh my Godfather
OMGN - Oh my God noob
OMGROFLMAO - Oh my God, rolling on the floor laughing my a** off
OMGWTFBBQ - Oh my gosh, what the F***in' barbeque
OMGYG2BK - Oh my God, you got to be kidding
OMGYS - Oh my God you suck
OMH - Oh my heavens!
OMJ - Oh my Jonas

OMIF - Open Mouth, Insert Foot
OML - Oh My Lord
OMM - On my mind
OMOHOD - One minute, one hour, one day
OMW - On my way
ONID - Oh No I Didn't
ONL - Online
ONNA - Oh No, Not Again
ONNTA - Oh No, Not This Again
ONUD - Oh No You Didn't
ONYD - Oh No, You Didn't
OO - Over and out and/or On Order and/or OpenOffice
OOAK - One of a Kind
OOC - Out of character and/or Out Of Control
OOF - Out Of Facility
OOH - Out of here
OOI - Out Of Interest
OOM - Out of mana
OOO - Out Of Office
OOS - Out Of Stock
OOSOOM - Out of sight, Out of mind
OOT - Out Of Touch and/or Out Of Topic
OOTB - Out Of the Box and/or Out Of the Blue
OOTC - Obligatory On Topic Comment
OOTD - One of these days and/or Outfit of the Day
OOTO - Out of the office
OOYFM - Out of your f***ing mind
OP - On phone and/or Over Price and/or Original Poster
OPM - Other people's money
ORLY - Oh really?
OSIF - Oh Sh** I Forgot
OSINTOT - Oh Sh** I Never Thought Of That
OST - On Second Thought
OT - Off topic and/or On topic and/or Other Topic and/or Overtime

OTASOIC - Owing To A Slight Oversight In Construction
OTB - Off to bed and/or Off the Boat
OTC - Over the Counter
OTE - Over the edge
OTF - Off The Floor and/or On The phone (Fone)
OTFL - On the floor laughing
OTFLMAO - On the floor laughing my ass off
OTG - On the ground
OTGL - On the ground laughing
OTH - Off the Hook
OTL - Out to lunch
OTOH - On the other hand
OTOOH - On the Other Other Hand
OTP - On the phone
OTS - On the Scene and/or On the Spot and/or Off the Shelf and/or Off the Subject
OTT - Over the top
OTTH - On the third hand
OTTOMH - Off the top of my head
OTW - Off to work and/or Off the Wall and/or Outta this World and/or On the Way
OTFW - Outta this F***ing world
OTRW - Outta the real world
OTW - Off to work and/or on the way
OUSU - Oh, You Shut Up
OVA – Over
OWTTE - Or Words To That Effect
OYO - On your own
OZ - Australia

"Letter P"

P - Partner

P/W - Password

P&C - Private & Confidential

P&H - Parents at home

P-ZA – Pizza

P2C2E - Process Too Complicated Too Explain

P2P - Parent to parent and/or Peer to Peer and/or Pay to Play

P2U4URAQTP - Peace to You for You Are a Cutie Pie

P911 - Parents coming into room alert

PA – Parent Alert

PAB - Poor Ass Bastard

PABG - Packing a Big Gun

PAH - Parents at home

PAL - Parents Are Listening

PANS - Pretty Awesome New Stuff

PAT - Meaning "patrol" and/or Pitching a Tent

PAW - Parents are watching

PAX - Peace and Love

PB - Potty Break

PBB - Parent behind Back

PBEM - Play by Email

PBIAB - Pay Back Is a Bitch

PBJ - Peanut Butter and Jelly and/or Pretty Boy Jock

PBOOK - Phonebook (e-mail)

PC - Player character and/or Personal Computer and/or Politically Correct and/or Private Chat

PC4PC - Picture comment for picture comment

PCID - Putting clothes in dryer

PCM - Please call me

PCMCIA - People Can't Memorize Computer Industry Acronyms

PCT - Podcasting

PD - Public Domain

PDA - Personal display of affection and/or Public Display of Affection

PDH - Pretty damn happy and/or Pretty damn Hot

PDOMA - Pulled Directly Out Of My Ass

PDQ - Pretty damn quick

PDS - Please don't shoot and/or please don't shout

PEBCAC - Problem Exists Between Chair and Computer

PEBCAK - Problem Exists Between Chair and Keyboard

PEEP - People Engaged and Empowered for Peace

PEEPS – People

PFA - Pulled From Ass and/or Please Find Attached

PFC - Pretty F***ing Cold

PFM - Pure F***ing Magic

PFO - Pissed and fell over

PFR - Plasma, Frag, Rocket

PFT - Pretty F***ing tight

PG - Pretty good

phat - Pretty Hot And Tempting

PHB - Pointy Haired Boss

PHD - Pompous Headed Dweeb

PHS - Pointy Haired Stupidvisor

PIAM - Pleasure Is All Mine

PIAPS - Pig in a Pant Suit

PIBKAC - Problem Is Between Keyboard and Chair

PIC – Picture

PICNIC - Problem in Chair, Not In Computer

PIF - Paid In Full

PIMP – Peeing In My Pants

PIMPL - Peeing In My Pants Laughing

PIN - Person in Need

PIO - Pass it on

PIOG - Posted in other groups

PIP - Peeing in pants (laughing hard)

PIR - Parents in room and/or People in room

PISS - Put in some sugar

PITA - Pain in the Ass
PITMEMBOAM - Peace in the Middle East My Brother of another Mother
pix - pictures and/or photos
PJDWYS - Personal joke, don't worry yourself
PK - Preacher's Kid
PKMN - Pokémon
PL – Pig Latin and/or Play List and/or Punch Line
PL& - Planned
PL8 - Plate
PLD – Played
PLJ - Peace, love, joy
PLMK - Please let me know
PLO - Peace, Love, Out
PLOKTA - Press Lots of Keys to Abort
PLOS - Parents Looking Over Shoulder
plox - Please
PLS - Please
PLU - People like us
PLZ - Please
PLZTLME - Please tell me
PM - Private Message and/or Personal Message and/or Postmeridian
PMBI - Pardon My Butting In
PMD – Paid My Dues and/or Paying My Dues
PMF - Pardon My French and/or Pure Freaking Magic
PMFI - Pardon me for interrupting
PMFJI - Pardon me for jumping in
PMIGBOM - Put Mind in Gear before Opening Mouth
PMJI - Pardon My Jumping In
PML - Pissing Myself Laughing
PMP - Peed My Pants
PMPL - Piss my pants laughing
PMSL - Pee myself laughing
PMWOF - Putting more wood on the fire

PNAR - Poppin and a ranging
PNATMBC - Pay No Attention to Man Behind the Curtain
PNATTMBTC - Pay No Attention to the Man Behind the Curtain
PNCAH - Please, No Cursing Allowed Here
PND - Possibly Not Definitely and/or Personal Navigation Device
PNP - Plug and Play
PO - Piss Off
POAHF - Put on a happy face
POAK - Passed Out At Keyboard
POC - Piece of Crap and/or Point of Contact
poed - P*ssed off
POMS - Parent over My Shoulder
PONA - Person of No Account
POOF - Left the chatroom in a puff of smoke
POP - Photo on Profile, Point of Purchase, Point Of Presence, Post Office Protocol
POS - Parent over shoulder and/or Piece of Sh** and/or Power of Suggestion
posbl - Possible
POSC - Piece Of Sh** Computer
POSSLQ - Persons of the Opposite Sex Sharing Living Quarters
pot - Potion
POTATO - Person over Thirty Acting Twenty One
POTB - Pat on the back
POTC - Peck on the cheek and/or Pirates of the Caribbean
POTO - Pointing Out the Obvious and/or Phantom of the Opera
POTS - Plain Old Telephone System and/or Pat on the Shoulder
POTUS - President of the United States
POV - Point of view and/or Privately Owned
PP – People and/or Pause Please

PPDA - Parents pacing de area
PPL – Pay-Per-Lead and/or People
PPU - Pending pick-up
PPV - Pay-Per-View
PRL - Parents are listening
PROLLY – Probably
PROGGY - Meaning computer program
PRON - Meaning pornography
PRT – Party and/or Please Retweet (Twitter slang)
prvt - Private
PRW - People/parents are watching
PRY - Probably and/or pretty
PS - Post Script
PSA - Public Service Announcement
PSO - Product Superior to Operator
PSOG - Pure stroke of genius
PSOS - Parent standing over shoulder
PSP - PlayStation Portable
PST - Please send tell
PTB - Powers to be
PTH - Prime Tanning Hours
PTIYPASI - Put that in your pipe and smoke it
PTL - Praise the Lord
PTM - Please tell me
PTMM - Please tell me more
PTO - Pass this on
PTP - Pardon the Pun
PTPOP - Pat the Pissed Off Primate
PTSB - Pass the sick bucket
PU - That Stinks
PUG - Pick up group
PUKS - Pick up kids (SMS)
PUSIMP - Put yourself in my position
puter – computer
PUYD – Pick up your daughter

PUYS – Pick up your son
PVP - Player versus player
pvt - Private
pw – Password
PWAS - Prayer Wheels Are Spinning
PWCB - Person Will Call Back
pwn - Own
pwnt – Owned
PWOF - Putting wood on the fire
PWP - Plot, What Plot?
PWT - Poor white trash
PXT - Please explain that
PYHOOYA - Pull your head out of your ass
PYSIMP - Put yourself in my place
PYT - Pretty young thing
PZ - Peace
PZA - Pizza

"Letter Q"
Q – Queue and/or Question
Q2C - Quick To Cum
Q4U - Question for you
QC - Quality control
QFE - Question for everyone
QFI - Quoted for idiocy and/or Quoted for Irony
QFT - Quoted For Truth and/or Quit F***ing Talking
QIK - Quick
QL - Quit laughing
QLS - Reply
QOTD - Quote of the day
QQ (qq) - Meaning "crying eyes"
QQ - Quick question
qqn - Looking
QS - Quit Scrolling
QSL - Reply

QSO - Conversation
QT – Cutie and/or Q Tip and/or Quality Time
QTPI - Cutie pie
QYB - Quit Your Bitching

"Letter R"
R – Are
R&D - Research & Development
R&R - Rest & Relaxation
R8 - Rate (SMS)
RAEBNC - Read and Enjoyed, But No Comment
RAF - Ready, Aim, Fire
RAK - Random act of kindness
RAT - Remotely Activated Trojan
rawr - Roar
RB@YA - Right Back at Ya
RBAY - Right back at you
RBJ – Really Bad Joke
RBTL - Read Between the Lines
RC - Remote Control
RCI - Rectal Cranial Inversion
RDF - Real deal feeling
rdnk - Redneck
rdy - Ready
RE - Regards and/or Reply and/or Hello Again and/or
Resident Evil
REHI - Hi Again
REW - Right Ear Worthy
RFC - Request for Comments
RFD - Request for Discussion
RFN - Right F***ing now
RFP - Request for Proposal
RFR - Really F***ing Rich
RFS - Really F***ing Soon
rgd - Regard

RGR - Roger
RHIP - Rank has its privileges
RHK - RoundHouse Kick
RIMJS - Really I'M Just Saying
RIP - Rest in peace
RIYL - Recommended If You Like
RKBA - Right to Keep and Bear Arms
RL - Real life
RLAD - Read, love and die
RLCO - Real Life Conference
RLF - Real Life Friend
RLY – Really
RM – Remake
RmbaYaMne - Remember You're Mine
RME - Rolling my eyes
RMETTH - Rolling My Eyes to the Heavens
RMLB - Read my lips baby
RMMA - Reading My Mind Again
RMMM - Read my mail man
RN - Right Now and/or Run
RNN - Reply Not Necessary
rnt – Aren't
ROBL - Rolling on back laughing
ROF - Rolling on floor
ROFL - Rolling on floor laughing and/or Rolling over F***in' laughing
ROFLAS - Rolling On Floor Laughing and Screaming
ROFLCOPTER - Rolling on floor laughing and spinning around
ROFLMAO - Rolling on the floor, laughing my Ass off
ROFLOL - Rolling on the floor laughing out loud
ROI - Return on Investment
ROLF - Rolling on laughing floor
ROLMBO - Rolling over laughing my butt off
ROM - Rough order of magnitude

ROR - Raffing out Roud (in scooby-doo dialect)
ROTF - Rolling On the Floor
ROTFL - Rolling on the floor laughing
ROTFLH - Rolling on the floor laughing hysterically
ROTFLMAOTID - Rolling On the Floor Laughing My Ass Off Till I Die
ROTFLMFAO - Rolling On the Floor Laughing My F***ing Ass Off
ROTFLMOA - Rolling On the Floor Laughing My Ass Off
ROTFLMOB - Rolling on the floor, laughing my butt off
ROTFLOL - Rolling On the Floor Laughing Out Loud
ROTFLOLAPMP - Rolling On the Floor Laughing Out Loud and Peeing My Pants
ROTFLTIC - Rolling On the Floor Laughing Till I Cry
ROTFLUTS - Rolling on the floor laughing unable to speak
ROTFWTIME - Rolling on the floor with tears in my eyes
ROTGL - Rolling On the Ground Laughing
ROTGLMOA - Rolling On the Ground Laughing My Ass Off
ROTM - Right On the Money
ROTS - Right on the spot
RP – Role Playing
RPG - Role Playing Games
RRQ - Return Receipt reQuested
RRR - haR haR haR (instead of LOL)
RS - Runescape
RSN - Real soon now
RSVP - Repondez S'il Vous Plait
RT - Roger that and/or Retweet (Twitter slang) and/or Real Time
RTBS - Reason to be single
RTBM - Read the Bloody Manual
rtf - Return the favor
RTFA - Read the f***in' article
RTFAQ - Read the Frequently Asked Questions

RTFB - Read the f***in' book
RTFF - Read the F***ing FAQ
RTFM - Read the F***ing manual
RTFQ - Read the F***ing question
RTG - Ready to Go
RTH - Release the Hounds
RTI - Real-Time Interruption
RTK - Return to Keyboard
RTM - Read the Manual
RTMS - Read the manual, stupid
RTNTN - Retention
RTRCTV - Retroactive
RTRMT - Retirement
RTS - Real-time strategy
RTSM - Read the stupid manual
RTSS - Read the Screen Stupid
RTTSD - Right Thing to Say Dude
RTWFQ - Read the whole F***ing question
RTWT - Read the Whole Thing
RU - Are you?
RU/18 - Are You Over 18?
RUB - Are you back
RUC - Are you coming?
RUCB - Are you coming back?
RUCMNG - Are you coming?
r u da? - Are You There
RUFKM - Are You F***ing Kidding Me?
RUFR - Are you for real
r u goin - are you going?
RUH - Are You Horny?
RUMCYMHMD - Are You on Medication Cause You Must Have Missed a Dose
RUMORF - Are You Male OR Female?
RUN - Are you in?
RUNTS - Are You Nuts

RUT - Are u (you) there?
RUOK - Are you okay?
RUS - Are You Serious?
RUSOS - Are You SOS (in trouble)?
RUT - Are You There?
RUUP4IT - Are You Up For It?
RU\18 - Are You under 18?
RX - Regards
RW - Real world
RWA - Ready, Willing, and Able
RX - Meaning drugs or prescriptions
RYB - Read your Bible
RYFM - Read Your Friendly Manual and/or Read Your
F***ing Manual
RYFS - Are you F***in' serious?
RYO - Roll your own
RYS - Read your screen and/or Are you Single?

"Letter S"
S – Smiling and/or Yes
S^ - what's up?
S~! - Salute
S'OK - Meaning It' (s) okay (ok)
S2R - Send to receive
S2S - Sorry to say
S2U - Same to You
S4B - Sh** for Brains
S4L - Spam for Life
SADAD - Suck A Dick and Die
SAHM - Stay at Home Mom
SAIA - Stupid Asses in Action
SAL - Such a laugh
SALAB - Stop acting like a baby
SAMAGAL - Stop annoying me and get a life
samzd - Still amazed

SAPFU - Surpassing All Previous F*** Ups
SASE - Self-addressed stamped envelope
SAT - Sorry about that and/or Scholastic Aptitude Test
SB – Stand By and/or Should Be and/or Smiling Back
SBI - Sorry 'Bout It
SBT - Sorry 'bout that
SBTA - Sorry, Being Thick Again
SBTM - Should be there momentarily
SBUG - Small Bald Unaudacious Goal
SC - Stay cool
SCNR - Sorry, Could Not Resist
SDIHTT - Someday I'll have the time
SDK - Scottie Doesn't Know and/or Software Developer's Kit
SDMB - Sweet dreams, my baby
SEAL - Slaying everyone and laughing
sec - wait a second
SED – Said Enough Darling
SEG – Sh** Eating Grin
SEP - Somebody Else's Problem
SETE - Smiling Ear-to-Ear
SEWAG - Scientifically Engineered Wild Ass Guess
SF - Surfer Friendly and/or Science Fiction
SFAIAA - So Far As I Am Aware
SFAIK - So far as I know
SFB - S*** for brains
SFE2E - Smiling from ear to ear
SFETE - Smiling From Ear To Ear
SFF - So F***ing funny
SFLA – Stupid Four Letter Acronym
SFTTM - Stop F***ing Talking To Me
SFX - Sound Effects and/or Stage Effects
SFY - Speak for yourself
SH - Sh** Happens and/or Same Here
SH^ - Shut up
SHB - Should Have Been

shhh - Quiet
SHID - Slapping head in disgust
SHMILY - See How Much I Love You
SIA - Someone is around
SIC - Spelling Is Correct
SICL - Sitting In Chair Laughing
SICNR - Sorry, I could not resist
SICS - Sitting In Chair Snickering
SIG - Silence is golden
SIG2R - Sorry, I got to run
SIHTH - Stupidity is hard to take
SII - Seriously Impaired Imagination
SIL - Sister-In-Law and/or Son-in-law
SIM - Shoot, its Monday
SIMYC - Sorry I missed your call
SINBAD - Single income, no boyfriend, absolutely desperate
SIP - Skiing In Powder
SIR - Strike it rich
SIS - Snickering in silence
SIT - Stay in touch
SITCOM - Single Income, Two Children, Oppressive Mortgage
SITD - Still In the Dark
siul8r - See you later
SIUP - Suck It Up Pussy
SIUYA - Shove It Up Your Ass
SK8 - Skate
SK8NG - Skating
SK8R - Skater
SK8RBOI - Skater Boy
SL - Second Life
SLAP - Sounds like a plan
SLAW - Sounds Like a Winner
SLIRK - Smart Little Rich Kid
SLM - See Last Mail

SLOM - Sticking Leeches on Myself
SLT - Something like That
SLY - Still love you
SM - Senior Moment
SMAIM - Send Me an Instant Message
SMB - Suck My Balls
SMDH - Shaking my D*** head
SME - Subject Matter Expert
SMEM - Send Me E-Mail
SMF - So much fun
SMH - Scratching my head and/or Shaking my head
SMHID - Scratching my head in disbelief
SML - So much love
SMOP - Small Matter of Programming
SMOT - Support Me on This
smt - Something
SNAFU - Situation normal all F***ed up
SNAG - Sensitive New Age Guy
SNERT - Snot nosed egotistical rude teenager
SNMP - So not my problem
SNU - Sender needs you
SO - Significant other
SO8 - Sweet
SOAB - Son of a Bitch
SOB - Stressed Out Bigtime and/or Son of a Bitch
SOBT - Stressed Out Big Time
SODDI - Some Other Dude Did It
SOE - Start of Exams
SOGOP - Sh** or Get Off the Pot
SOH - Sense of Humor
SOHF - Sense of Humor Failure
SOI - Self Owning Idiot
SOIAR - Sit On It and Rotate
SOL - Sooner or later and/or Sh** Out of Luck
sok – it's ok

some1 - someone
SOMY - Sick of me yet?
SOOI - Stay out of it
SOOYA - Snake Out Of Your Ass
SOP - Standard Operating Procedure
SorG - Straight or Gay?
SOS - Meaning help and/or Same Old Sh** and/or Son of Sam and/or Same Old Stuff and/or Someone Special and/or Someone over Shoulder
SOSG - Someone over shoulder gone
SOSO - Same old, same old
SOT - Short of time
SOTA - State of the Art
SOTMG - Short of time, must go
SOW - Speaking Of Which and/or Statement of Work and/or Scope of Work
SOWM - Someone with me
soz – Sorry
SPAM - Stupid Person's AdvertiseMent
SPK - Speak (SMS)
SPKR – Speaker
SPROS - Stop, parents reading over shoulder
SRO - Standing Room Only
SRSLY - Seriously
SPST - Same place, same time
SPTO - Spoke to
SQ – Square
SRO - Standing room only
srsly - Seriously
SRY - Sorry
SS - So sorry
SSC - Super Sexy Cute
SSDD - Same Sh**, different day
SSEWBA - Someday Soon, Everything Will Be Acronyms
SSIA - Subject Says It All

SSIF - So stupid it's funny
SSINF - So stupid it's not funny
ST&D - Stop texting and drive
ST2M - Stop talking to me
STAR - Stop, think, act, review
STBX - Soon To Be Ex
STBY - Sucks To Be You
STD - Seal the Deal and/or Save the Date and/or Sexually Transmitted Disease
STFD - Sit the f*** down and/or Shut the front door
STFU - Shut the F*** up
STFW - Search the F***ing Web
sth – something
STHU - Shut the hell up
STLSDR - Still too long, still didn't read
STM - Spank the Monkey
STMS - Sick to my stomach
STN - Spend the Night
STPPYNOZGTW - Stop Picking Your Nose, Get To Work
STR8 – Straight
STS - So To Speak
STTH - Speak to the hand
STW - Search the Web
STYS - Speak To You Soon
SU - Shut Up
SUAC - Sh** Up A Creek
SUAFU - Situation unchanged, all f***ed up
SUAKM - Shut Up and Kiss Me
SUF - Shut your face
SUFI - Super Finger and/or Shut up F***ing Imbecile
SUFID - Screwing Up Face in Disgust
SUITM - See you in the morning
SUL - See you later and/or Snooze You Loose
SUM1 - Someone
SUP - What's up?

SUSFU - Situation unchanged, still fouled up

SUTH - So use (d) to haters (Facebook)

SUV - Stupid, Useless Vehicle

SUX - Meanings sucks or "it sucks"

SUYF - Shut Up You Fool

SvnALMyLuv4U - Saving All My Love for You

SWA - So what ass

SWAG - Scientific Wild Ass Guess and/or SoftWare and Giveaways and/or Something We All Get

SWAK - Sent (or sealed) with a kiss

SWALBCAKWS - Sealed With a Lick Because A Kiss Won't Stick

SWALK - Sealed with a loving kiss and/or Sweet, with all love, kisses

SWAS - Said with a smile

SWAT - Scientific wild Ass guess

SWDYT - So What Do You Think?

SWDYWTTA - So what do you want to talk about?

sweet<3 – sweetheart

SWF - Single White Female

SWIM - See What I Mean?

SWIS - See What I'm Saying

SWL - Screaming with laughter

SWMBO - She who must be obeyed

SWU - So What's Up?

SY - Sincerely yours

SYG – SYG - Screwing you get (for the) screwing you gave

SYIH - See you in h***

SYL - See you later

SYLA - See you later alligator

SYS - See you soon

SYT - See You Tomorrow

SYY - Shut your yapper

"Letter T"

T&C - Terms & Conditions

T@YL - Talk at You Later

T+ - Think positive

T2U - Talk to you

T2UL - Talk to You Later

T2UT - Talk to You Tomorrow

T2YL - Talk to you later

T4BU - Thanks for being you

T:)T - Think happy thoughts

TA - Thanks a lot and/or Thanks Again

TAB - Talking about

TABOOMA - Take A Bite Out Of My Ass

TAC - Times are changing and/or That Ain't Cool

TAF - That's All, Folks

TAFN - That's all for now

TAH - Take A Hike

TAKS - That's a Knee Slapper

TAM - Tomorrow a.m. and/or Thanks a Million

TANJ - There Ain't No Justice

TANK - Meaning really strong

TANKED - Meaning "owned"

TANKING - Meaning "owning"

TANSTAAFL - There Ain't No Such Thing as A Free Lunch

TAP - Take a Pill

TARFU - Things Are Really F***ed Up

TAS - Taking a Shower

TAT - This and that

TAU - Thinking about u (you)

TAUMUALU - Thinking about you miss you always love you

TAW - Teachers Are Watching

TAY - Thinking about you

TB - Titty Bar

TBA - To Be Advised and/or To be announced

TBC - To be continued
TBCL - To be continued later
TBD - To be determined and/or To be decided
TBE - To be edited
TBF - To be fair and/or To be frank
TBH - To be honest
TBL - Text back later
TBY - Teacher behind you
TBYB - Try Before You Buy
TC - Take care and/or That's cool
TCB - Take care of business and/or Trouble came back
TCCIC - Take care 'cause I care
TCO - Total Cost of Ownership
TCOB - Takin' care of business
TCOOD - Taking clothes out of dryer
TCOY - Take Care Of Yourself
TCWB - Take care, write back
TDL - The Do LaB
TDM - Too Darn Many
TDTM - Talk Dirty To Me
TED - Totally EavesDropping
tel – Telephone
teme - Tell me
TEOTWAWKI - The End of the World As We Know It
TFB - Too f***kin' bad
TFDS - That's For Darn Sure
TFF - Too f***kin' funny
TFH - Thread from Hell
TFLMS - Thanks for Letting Me Share
TFM - Thanks from Me
TFMIU - The F***ing Manual Is Unreadable
TFN - Thanks for Nothing and/or Til Further Notice
TFS - Thanks for Sharing and/or Three Finger Salute
TFTHOAT - Thanks for the Help Ahead Of Time
TFTI - Thanks for the information

TFTT - Thanks for the Thought
TFX – Traffic
TFYS - The F*** You Say
TG - Thank goodness
TGAL - Think Globally, Act Locally
TGGTG - That Girl/Guy has got to go
TGIF - Thank God It's Friday
TH - Tears of happiness
THNX - Thanks
THNQ - Thank-you (SMS)
THTH - Too hot to handle
THX - Thanks
THT - Think happy thoughts
tht - That
TIA - Thanks in advance
TIAD - Tomorrow is another day
TIAIL - Think I Am In Love
TIC - Tongue-in-cheek
TIGAS - Think I Give A Sh**
TILII - Tell It Like It Is
TILIS - Tell it like it is
TIME - Tears in My Eyes
TINGTES - There Is No Gravity, the Earth Sucks
TINWIS - That Is Not What I Said
TIPS - To improve professional service
TIR - Teacher in room
TISC - This Is So Cool
TISL - This Is So Lame
TISNC - This Is So Not Cool
TISNF - That Is So Not Fair
TISNT - That Is So Not True
TISU - This is so unfair
TITF - That is too funny
TJI - Try joining in
TK - To Come

TKA - Totally Kick A**

TKU4UK - Thank You for Your Kindness

TL - Too long

TLA - Three Letter Acronym

TLC - Tender Loving Care

TLDR - Too long, didn't read

TLGO - The List Goes On

TLITBC - That's Life in the Big City

TLK2UL8R - Talk to you later

TM - Trust Me and/or Trouble Maker and/or Tell Me and/or Tickle Me and/or Trademark

TMA - Take my advice and/or To many Acronyms

TMAI - Tell me about it

TMB - Text me back and/or Tweet me back and/or Tag me back

TMDF - To my dearest friend

TMFT - Too much free time

TMG - That's my girl

TMI - Too much information

TMOT - Trust me on this

TMS - Touch my soul

TMSF - Too much Science Fiction

TMSOG - Too Much Sh** Going On

TMTH - Too much to handle

TMTOWTDI - There's More Than One Way to Do It

TMWFI - Take my word for it

TNA - Temporarily Not Available

TNC - Tongue in Cheek

TNG - The Next Generation

TNSTAAFL - There's no such thing as a free lunch

TNT - Till next time

TNTL - Trying Not To Laugh

TNX – Thanks

TNXE6 - Thanks a Million

TOBAL - There Oughta Be A Law

TOBG - This Oughta Be Good
TOD - Truth or dare
TOH - The other half and/or typing one-handed
TOIOM - This one is on me
TOJ - Tears of joy
TOL - Thinking of laughing
TOM – Tomorrow
TOMA - Take over My Arse/Ass
TOPCA - Til Our Paths Cross Again
TOS - Terms of service
TOT - Tons of Time
TOU and/or TOY - Thinking of you
TOW - The one with and/or The one where
TOWL - The one with love
TOY - Thinking of you
TP - Team Player and/or TelePort and/or Turn Pale
TPC - The Phone Company
TPM - Tomorrow PM
TPS - That's Pretty Stupid
TPT - Trailor Park Trash
TPTB - The powers that be and/or the powers to be
TQ - Te quiero / I love you (Spanish SMS) and/or Thank You
TQM - Total Quality Management
TQVM - Thank you very much
TRAM - The Rest Are Mine
TRBL - Terrible
TRDMC - Tears Running Down My Cheeks
TRDMF - Tears running down my face
tripdub - triple w
troo - true
TRP - Television Rating Points
TRS - That really sucks
TS - Tough Sh** and/or Totally Stinks
TSH - Tripping so hard
TSIA - This Says It All

TSIF - Thank Science It's Friday
TSNF - That's so not fair
TSOB - Tough Son Of a Bitch
TSR - Totally Stuck in RAM and/or Totally Stupid Rules
TSRA - Two Shakes of a Rat's Ass
TSS - This stuff sucks and/or Toxic Shock Syndrome
TSTB - The sooner, the better
TSTL - Too stupid to live
TT - Big Tease and/or Till Tomorrow and/or Talk too
TT2T - Too tired to talk
TT4N - Ta-ta for now
TTA - Tap That Ass
TTBOMK - To the Best of My Knowledge
TTFN – Ta-Ta for now
TTG - Time to Go
TTIOT - The Truth Is Out There
TTKA - Time to kick ass
TTKSF - Trying To Keep a Straight Face
TTL - Talk to you later and/or Time to leave and/or Time to Live
TTM – Talk To Me
TTMF – Ta-Ta MOFO
TTLY – Totally
TTPECC - There's a Time and a Place for Everything
TTS - Text To Speech
TTT - That's the Ticket and/or To the Top and/or Thought That Too
TTTH - Talk to the Hand
TTTHTFAL - Talk to the Hand the Face Ain't Listening
TTTKA - Time to Totally Kick Ass
TTTT - These things take time and/or Too tired to talk and/or To tell the truth
TTUL - Talk to you later
TTY - Talk to you
TTYAW - Talk to you after work

TTYAWFN - Talk to You A While From Now
TTYAFN - Talk to you awhile from now
TTYIAB - Talk to you in a bit
TTYIAF - Talk/Type to You in a Few
TTYIAM - Talk to you in a minute
TTYL - Talk to You Later and/or Type to You Later
TTYLMF - Talk to you later, my friend
TTYN - Talk to you never
TTYOOTD - Talk to you one of these days
TTYS - Talk to You Soon
TTYT - Talk to You Tomorrow
TTYVS - Talk to you very soon
TTYW - Talk to you whenever
TU - Thank you
TUI - Turning you in
TUT - Totally unique thought
TUVM - Thank you very much
TVM4YEM - Thank You Very Much For Your E-Mail
TWHAB - This Won't Hurt A Bit
TWHE - The Walls Have Ears
TWHS - That's what he said
TWIMC - To Whom It May Concern
TWIS - That's what I said
TWIT - That's what I thought
TWITA - That's What I'm Talking About
TWIWI - That Was Interesting, Wasn't It?
TWMA - Till we meet again
TWSI - That was so ironic
TWSS - That's what she said
TWTI - That was totally ironic
tx - Thanks
TXS – Thanks
TXT IM - Text Instant Message
TXT MSG - text message
TY - Thank you

TYCLO - Turn Your CAPS LOCK Off
TYFC - Thank you for charity
TYFYC - Thank you for your comment
TYG - There You Go
TYL - Thank you Lord
TYM - Thank you much
TYS - Told you so
TYT- Take your time
TYSO - Thank you so much
TYAFY - Thank you and F*** you
TYVM - Thank you very much

"Letter U"
^URS - Up yours
U2 - You Too
U2U - Up to you
u8 - you ate?
u – You
u up - are you up?
UAD - You are drunk
UBD - User brain damage
UBS - Unique Buying State
UCE - Unsolicited commercial e-mail
UCMU - You crack me up
UCWAP - Up a Creek without a Paddle
UDFI - You don't fit in
UDH82BME - You'd hate to Be Me
UDI - Unidentified drinking injury (meaning bruise, scratch, ache and so on)
UDM - U (You) da (the) man
UDS - Ugly domestic scene
UFB - UN F***ing believable
UFC - Unregistered Fat Chick
UFN - Until further notice
UG2BK - You've got to be kidding

UGC - User-Generated Content
UKTR - You know that's right
UKWIS - You know what I'm saying
UL – Upload and/or Unlucky
U-L - Meaning "You will"
ULKGR8 - You look great
UMMC - You make me crazy
UMML - You make me laugh
UNA - Use no acronyms
UNADR - You need a doctor
UNAST - You need a special training
UN4TUN8 - Unfortunate
UNBLEFBLE - Unbelievable
UNCRTN – Uncertain
UNOIT - You Know It
UNPC - UN- (not) politically correct
UNTCO - You Need to Chill Out
UOK - (Are) you ok?
UOM - You Owe Me
UOMBT - You Owe Me Big Time
UOME - You owe me
UPI - Unidentified Party Injury
UPOD - You Need to Chill Out
UR - You are / you're
UR2K - You Are Too Kind
UR2M - You are too much
UR2YS4ME - You are too wise for me
URA* - You are a star
URAB - You are a bitch and/or you are a Boob
URAL - You are a loser
URAPITA - You Are A Pain in the Ass
URAQT - You are a cutie
ure - You're
URGR8 - You are great
URH - You are hot (U R Hot)

URL – You are Lazy
URSIA - You Are Such an Idiot
URSKTM - You are so kind to me
URTM - You are the man
URW - You are welcome
URWS - You Are Wise
URYY4M - You Are Too Wise For Me
URZ – yours
USA - Until sides ache and/or United States of America
USAD - You're such a dork and/or You're such a Dick
USB - You sexy bitch and/or You sexy Bastard
USBCA - Until something better comes along
USP - Unique Selling Proposition
USU - Usually
UT - Unreal Tournament and/or You There?
UT2L - You take too long
UTM - You tell me
UV - Unpleasant visual
UW - You're welcome
UWIWU - You Wish I Was You
UY – Up Yours

"Letter V"
VBG - Very Big Grin
VBS - Very big smile
VC - Venture Capital and/or Voice Chat
VCDA – Vaya Con Dios, Amigo
VE - Very emotional
VEG - Very evil grin
VFF - Very freaking funny
VFM - Value for money
VGC - Very good condition
VGG - Very good game
VGH - Very good hand
VGN - Vegan -or- Vegetarian

VIFI - Very Important Food Item
VIM - Very Important Member
VIP - Very important person
VIV - Very Important Visitor
VM - Voice mail
VN - Very nice
VNH - Very nice hand
VRBS - Virtual Reality Bull Sh**
VRY - Very
VSC - Very soft chuckle
VSF - Very sad face
VURP - Vomit-burp
VVB - Very, Very Back
VWD - Very well done
VWP - Very well played

"Letter W"
w wult - what would you like to talk about
W@ - What?
w's^ - what's up?
W/ - With
W/B - Welcome back
W00T - We Own the Other Team and/or Joy and excitement and/or Amazing, cool
W2F - Way too funny
W2G - Way to go
W3 - WWW (Web address)
w4m - women for men
W4U - Waiting for you
W8 – Wait
W84M - Wait for me
w8n - Waiting
W9 - Wife in room
wa - What
WABOC - What a Bunch of Crap

WAD - Without a Doubt
WADITWB - We always did it that way before
WADR - With all due respect
WAEF - When All Else Fails
WAEFRD - When all else fails, read directions
WAFB - What A F***ing Bitch
WAFI - Wind Assisted F***ing Idiots
WAFM - What A F***ing Mess
WAFS - Warm and Fuzzies
WAFU - What A F*** Up
WAG - Wild Ass Guess
waggro - Wife aggro
WAHM - Work at home mom
WAI - What an Idiot
WAJ - What a jerk
WAJABOFU - We Are Just A Bunch of F*** Ups
WAK - What a Kiss
WAM - Wait a minute
WAMBAM - Web Application Meets Brick and Mortar
WAN2 - Want to?
WAN2TLK - Want to talk
WAREZ - meaning pirated (illegally gained) software
WAS - Wait a second
wat - What
WAWA - Where are we at?
WAY - Who are you? and/or What about You?
WAYD - What Are You Doing?
WAYDRN - What are you doing right now?
WATDT - What are you doing tonight?
WAYF - Where are you from?
WAYN - Where Are You Now?
WB - Write back and/or Welcome Back and/or Way Bored
WBP – Write Back Please
WBS - Write back soon
WBU - What about you?

WBW - With best wishes
WBWYC - Write back when you can
WC – Welcome and/or Who Cares
WCA - Who cares anyway?
WCMTSU - We Can't Make This Sh** Up
WD - Well Done
WDALYIC - Who Died And Left You In Charge?
WDDD - Woopie Doo Da Dey
WDMB - Will do my best
WDR - With Due Respect
WDT - Who Does That?
WDUMBT - What do you mean by that?
WDUW - What do you want?
WDYM - What Do You Mean?
WDYMBT - What Do You Mean By That?
WDYK - What do you know?
WDYS - What Did You Say?
WDYT - What Do You Think?
W/E - Whatever
W/END and/or W/E - Weekend
WE – Whatever
WEG - Wicked Evil Grin
WEI - Whatever idiot
WEML - Whatever major loser
WEP - Weapon
WETSU - We Eat This Sh** Up
WEU - What's eating you?
WF - Way Fun
WFM - Works for Me
WG - Wicked Grin
WGAFF - Who Gives A Flying F***
WGMGD - What Gets Measured Gets Done
WH5 - Who, what, when, where, why
wht – What
WHT - What Happened To and/or Whatever Happened To

111

WHYBAD - Where have you been all day?
WHYBATT - Where have you been all this time?
WIBAMU - Well, I'll Be a Monkey's Uncle
WIBNI - Wouldn't it be nice if
WIIFM - What's In It for Me?
WIIFY - What's In It for You?
WILB - Workplace Internet Leisure Browsing
WILCO - Will Comply
WIM - Woe Is Me
WIMC - Where is my car?
WIP - Work in Process
wirld - world
WISP - Winning is so pleasurable
WIT - Wordsmith in Training
WITFITS - What In the F*** Is This Sh**
WITP - What is the point?
WITR - Who's in the room?
WITW - What in the world
WIU - Wrap it up
WK - Week
WKD – Weekend and/or Wicked
wkrewl - way cool
WL - Whatta loser
WLMIRL - Would Like to Meet In Real Life
WLOL - Whip laugh out loud
WMAO - Working my ass off
WMB - Write me back
WMHGB - Where Many Have Gone Before
WMMOWS - Wash My Mouth Out With Soap
WMPL - Wet My Pants Laughing
WN - Why not
WNDITWB - We never did it this way before
WNOHGB - Where No One Has Gone Before
W/O - Without
WOA - Work Of Art**

WOC - Woman of Character
WOG - Wise Old Guy and/or Walk and Jog
WOHM - Working outside home mom
WOM - Word Of Mouth and/or Word of Mouse
WOMBAT - Waste of Money, Brains and Time
WOOF - Well Off Older Folks
WOOT - We Own the Other Team and/or Yay and/or Way out of topic and/or Waste of our time
WOP - With Out Papers
WOPE - Word Wipe
word - it means cool, a.k.a. word up
WOS - Walk of Shame and/or Wife over Shoulder
WOT – What and/or Waste of Time
WOTAM - Waste of Time and Money
WOTD - Word of the Day and/or Workout of the Day
WOTLK - Wrath of the Lich King
WOW - World of Warcraft
woz - Worry
WP - Well Played and/or Wrong Person
wrisit - Where is it
WRK - Work
WRT - With Regard To and/or With Respect To
wru - where are you?
WRU@ - Where are you at?
WRUD - What are you doing?
WRUDATM - What Are You Doing At the Moment
wsp - Whisper
WT - Without Thinking and/or What the and/or Who The
WTB - Want to buy
WTBH - What the bloody hell
WTC - What the crap
WTF - What the F***?
WTFAY - Where the f*** are you?
WTFDYJS - What the F*** Did You Just Say?
WTFE - What the F*** ever

WTFGDA - Way to F***ing Go, Dumb Ass

WTFH - What The F***ing Hell

WTFIYP - What the F*** Is Your Problem?

WTFNF - What the F****n F***

WTFO - What the F***, over

WTFRU - Where the f*** are you?

WTFWYCM - Why The F*** Would You Call Me?

WTG - Way to go

WTG4a\\%/ - Want to Go For a Drink

WTG - Way to Go

WTGP - Want to go Private?

WTH - What the heck? and/or What the Hell

WTHDTM - What the hell does that mean?

WTHOW - White Trash Headline of the Week

WTHWT - What the hell was that?

WTM - Who's the man? and/or What Time

WTMI - Way Too Much Information

WTN - What Then Now? and/or Who Then Now?

WTS - Want to sell? and/or What's that Sh**? and/or What the Sh**

WTSDS - Where the Sun Don't Shine

WTSHTF - When the Sh** Hits the Fan

WTT - Want to trade?

WTTM - Without Thinking Too Much

wtv – Whatever

WTYAF - Who threw you a fish?

WU - What's up?

WUA - What's up anyway?

WUBU2 - What have you been up to?

WUCIWUG - What you see is what you get

WUD - What are you doing? and/or What's up, dog?

WUF - Where you from? And/or Wow, you're funny

WUGF - What up girlfriend

WUIGB - Wait until I get back

WUM - Watch Your Mouth

WUP - What's up?
WUU2 - What are you up to?
WUW - What u (you) want?
WUWH - Wish You Were Here
WUWHIMA - Wish You Were Here In My Arms
WUWT - What's up with that?
WUZ - Meaning "was"
wuz4dina - What's for dinner?
wuzup - what's up?
wv – With
WW - Wrong Way and/or Wrong Window and/or Well Won
WWI - What was it?
WWJD - What would Jesus do?
WWNC - Will wonders never cease?
WWSD - What Would Satan Do?
WWTFW - What's with this f***ed up world?
WWYC - Write when you can
WWYD - What Would You Do?
WWY - Where Were You?
WX - Weather
WYCM - Will you call me?
WYD - What (are) you doing? and/or Who's your Daddy
WYCM – Will You Call Me?
WYFM - Would You F*** Me?
WYGAM - When you get a minute
WYGISWYPF - What You Get Is What You Pay For
WYGOWM - Will you go out with me?
WYHAM - When you have a minute
WYLEI - When you least expect it
WYM - What do You Mean? And/or Watch your mouth
WYMM - Will you marry me?
wymyn – Woman
WYP - What's Your Problem?
WYRN - What's Your Real Name?
WYS - Whatever You Say and/or what's your Sign?

WYSAWYG - What You See Ain't What You Get
WYSILOB - What You See Is a Load of Bullocks
WYSIWYG - What you see is what you get
WYSLPG - What You See Looks Pretty Good
WYT - Whatever You Think
WYWH - Wish you were here

"Letter X"
X-1-10 - Meaning "Exciting"
X - Kiss
X! - Meaning "a typical woman"
XD - Meaning "really hard laugh and/or Laughing Out Loud
XDD - Laughing especially hard
xep – Except
xfer - Transfer
XGS - X-Girlfriend Syndrome
xit – Exit
xitb4ili - Exit before I lose it
XLNT - Excellent
XLR8 - Meaning "faster" or "going faster"
XME - Excuse Me
xp - Experience
XO - Kiss and Hug
XOXOXO - Hugs & Kisses
XOXOZZZ - Hugs and Kisses and Sweet Dreams
XQZT – Exquisite
XTC - Ecstasy
XYL - Ex-young lady, meaning wife
XYZ - Examine your zipper
XXOO - Kiss, Kiss, Hug, Hug
XXX - Kisses

"Letter Y"

Y? - Why?

Y! - Why

Y – Yawn and/or Yes

Y2K - You're too kind

YA – Yet another

YA yaya - Yet Another Ya-Ya (as in yo-yo)

YAA - Yet another acronym

YABA - Yet another bloody acronym

YABUT - yes-BUT

YACC - Yet another Calendar Company

YAFIYGI - You Asked For It You Got It

YAJWD - You Ain't Just Whistling Dixie

YAOTM - Yet Another off Topic Message

YAR - Yeah, right

YARLY - Ya, really?

YATB - You are the best

YATFM - You Are Too F***ing Much

YAUN - Yet another Unix Nerd

YAV - Yuppie Assault Vehicle

YBF - You've Been F***ed

YBIC - Your brother in Christ

YBL - You'll be sorry!

YBS - You'll be sorry

YBY - Yeah Baby Yeah

YBYSA - You Bet Your Sweet Ass

YCCOI - You can count on it

YCCOM - You can count on me

YCDBWYCID - You can't do business when your computer is down

YCHT - You can have them

YCLIU - You can look it up

YCMTSU - You Can't Make This Sh** Up

YCMU - You crack me up

YCT - Your Comment To

YD – Yesterday and/or Ya Dig?
YDI - You deserved it
YDKM - You Don't Know Me
YEPPIES - Young Experimenting Perfection Seekers
YER - Your
YF - Wife
YG - Young gentleman
YG2BJ - You've got to be joking
YGBK - You Gotta Be Kidding
YGLT - You're Gonna Love This
YGM - You've got mail
YGBSM - You Gotta Be Sh**ing me
YGG - You go girl
YGLT - You're Gonna Love This
YGM - You've Got Mail
YGTBK - You've got to Be Kidding
YGTBKM - You've got to be kidding me
YGTI - You Get the Idea?
YGWYPF - You Get What You Pay For
YHBT - You have been trolled
YHBW - You have been warned
YHL - You have lost
YHM - You Have Mail
YIC - Yours in Christ
YIU - Yes, I understand
YIWGP - Yes, I Will Go Private
YKHII - You know how it is
YKI - You know it
YKW - You know what
YKWIM - You Know What I Mean
YKWYCD - You know what you can do
YKYARW - You know you're A Redneck When
YKWIM - You know what I mean
YL - Young lady
YLH - Your Loving Husband

YLW - Your Loving Wife
YM - Your Mother and/or Young Man
YMAK - You May Already Know
YMAL - You Might Also Like
YMBJ - You must be joking
YMMD - You Make My Day and/or You Made My Day
YMMV - Your mileage may vary
YMSF - Your momma's so fat
YNK - You never know
YOOW - You're out of work
YOYO - You're On Your Own
YPML - You're pulling my leg
YR – Your and/or Yeah Right
YRAG - You are a geek
YRG - You are good
YRL - You are lame
YRYOCC - You're running your own cuckoo clock
YS - You Stinker and/or You Suck and/or Yours sincerely
YSAN - You're Such a Nerd
ysdiw8 - why should i wait?
YSIC - Your sister in Christ
YSJ - You're so jealin
YSK - You Should Know
YSW - Yeah sure whatever
YSYD - Yeah sure you do
YT - You there? and/or Your Turn
YTB - You're the best and/or Youth talk back
YTF - Why the F*** and/or What the F***
YTRNW - Yeah That's Right, Now What?
YTTL - You take too long
YTTM - You Talk Too Much
YTTT - You Telling the Truth?
YTG - You're the greatest
YUPPIES - Young Urban Professionals
YVW - You're very welcome

YW - You're welcome
YWHNB - Yes, we have no bananas
YWHOL - Yelling "woohoo" out loud
YWIA - You're Welcome In Advance
YWSYLS - You win some, you lose some
YY4U - Too Wise For You
YYSS - Yeah yeah, sure sure
YYSSW - Yeah, yeah, sure, sure, whatever

"Letter Z"
Z - Zero
Z - Z's are calling (meaning going to bed/sleep)
Z - Meaning "Said"
Z% - Zoo
zerg - To gang up on someone
ZH - Sleeping Hour
ZMG and/or ZOMG - Used in World of Warcraft to mean OMG (Oh My God)
ZOMG - Oh my gosh!
ZOT - Zero tolerance
ZUP - Meaning "What's up?"
ZZZZ - Sleeping (or bored)

Other Miscellaneous Slangs

A Couple two three - I guess this means two or three

Ankle Biter - Someone of little account, who criticizes others who are much better than she is, like a little dog that barks and jumps around, trying to bite people's ankles

Apple Knocker - a hick or redneck, someone who runs around in overalls and knocks apples off trees with a stick

Arm Candy - That exceptionally attractive and younger person walking with the older well-to-do person

Ass Butt - The last half-inch or so of beer at the bottom of a bottle that tastes terrible

Attention Whore - A person or housepet who is starved for attention to the point of being annoying

Baby Mama - mother of one's children who is usually not a spouse

Back-Asswards - doing something in the most ridiculously wrong order

Badonkadonk - someone that has a nice butt

Back - Bar room slang for a chaser

Ball-breaker - Pushy, irritating, or just plain bothersome, said especially of a female boss

Balls - It's an old wives' tale that testicles can be used to measure hot temperatures to within a few degrees. Hot as balls is around 100 degrees Fahrenheit; hotter than balls is anything hotter.

Bannock Slap - A full open handed slap, as in the kind used to knead bread

Bargle - To nearly vomit, but not quite; halfway between burping and barfing

Beavage - When a woman exposes her butt cheeks or butt crack, it's called beavage

Bebahama - Bitch behind my back

Beelzebug - Satan in the form of a mosquito or fly that gets into your bedroom at 3 in the morning and cannot be killed

Biatch - Use in polite company in place of bitch

Bimbob - Male equivalent of bimbo; i.e., a very good-looking, charming, or otherwise attractive young man--not valued for his intellectual prowess.

Biscuit - One who is cute

B.I.T. - Bitch in Training. Preteen or teenage female with way too much attitude

Bitched-out - Unable to perform certain actions expected of oneself and/or to yell and curse at someone, demean, demoralize

Bitchslap - From the stereotype of a pimp's demeaning and abusive treatment of his prostitutes, whom he refers to as his bitches

Bling - sparkly and gaudy jewelry

Blonde-moment - a blank facial expression

Blorf - A person who's idea of exercise is taking the beer bottles back to the store in exchange for fresh brew. Generally overweight and shapeless. He/she can be winded tying up a pair of shoes.

Blow-out - A painstakingly sculpted male hairdo that uses styling gel and a hair dryer to create a frozen wall of hair

Blunderwear - Underwear that has marks

Boo - a boyfriend or girlfriend

Boonkie or Boonky - The backside or rump area

Boot-'n'-toot - An adverse gastric event, as during a bout of stomach flu, in which the afflicted is simultaneously vomiting and passing gas

Booty blocker - an item of clothing (usually a long sleeve shirt or a sweater) that covers one's bottom, when you are feeling insecure about its size

Boregasm - A sudden eruption of (hyper) activity after an amount of time sitting around doing nothing, being bored. Often accompanied by yelling and screaming

Boz - A zit so big it should have a name

Brain-cramp - To suddenly forget whatever you were going to say in the middle of a sentence

Brat-wagon - A minivan
Breastacula - A name for a woman well-endowed with breasts
Brodown - boy's night out
Bromance - two men that are close friends but do not have sex with one another
Bruntile - Smelling completely and utterly putrid
Bubble - Your personal space, the small area that is around you
Burkup - a simultaneous burp and hiccup
Burr, brrr - The degree of discomfort to a person once it is determined that he or she is cold
Business Class - Refers to a woman with a large ass. The explanation of the phrase is that her ass would be too big to fit in coach
Busyhands - a person (usually male) who shows his love for his friends by letting his hands roam over his friend's body without permission. Often excused by drunkeness or feeling affectionate
Cable - Bulky gold chain
Cable-ten - Low budget, cheap, shameful, despicable, shoddy, inexpensive
Cack - Individuals who are of great arrogance, or who are wholly belonging to the mainstream society and laws of social conformity and use that to their advantage. Cacks are also identified as assholes or similar offensive names
Cack Chugula - A respectfully deprecating nickname usually bestowed upon those who excel in slothing, boozing, and story telling
Cakewalk - Easily done, same as a piece of cake
Calp - Used to point out a pair of nice legs without the owner of the legs knowing
Callow - To touch someone inappropriately
Camel Toe - The same as a wedgie, except it only happens to females, and is a front wedgy

Cankles - a condition where a person's calves are the same width as her ankles

Cat Fight - A fight between women who don't know how to fight, but just scratch at each other

Celluhang - The rear overhang on a chair

Chav - derogatory term for a teenager who works

Check vitals - to keep an eye on your emails, cell phone, voice mail and any other electronic device you have

Chickenhead - A woman who seeks men for their money

Chictionary - A man's black book of ladies' numbers

Choke N' Puke - Canadian's nickname for McDonalds

Chooch - A person who does something stupid by making a lame comment or a physical action without thinking first

Chuddy - Being round--but not fat

Circus sex - Unprotected sex, working without a safety net and/or unusual sex

Clean the closet - A phrase used by married couples when referring to the sex act. This allows one to discuss it without the taboo as only the people familiar with the term know what it really means

Clingon - A driver of another vehicle who increases her speed when you attempt to pass her

Code Red - This means that he or she is WAY HOT!

Coinkidink and/or Coinkydink – Coincidence and/or a strange happening, unusually odd

Comance - A relationship between two people who work at the same company

Come-See-Come-Saw - One or the other and/or either or

Compass - A computer student who happens to be an ass

Condominimum - A condom for the short

Cougar - an older woman who dates younger men

Coyote ugly - after a night of drinking you wake up next to someone you don't know that is so ugly you'd rather bite off your body part then wake up next to them

Crackberry - A nickname for the Blackberry, which is a phone and an addictive digital email gadget

Creep - To seek out a potential hook-up, preferably one who is under the influence of alcohol?

Crunk - hip-hop genre

Cupcaking - displaying affection out in public

Cuggin - Chunk of hard snot found in your nose

Cunny - a beautiful girl with attitude

Cut Grass - To steal someone's girlfriend

Cutsey-Pukesy - Something couples (especially new ones) do that they think is very cute but makes you want to hurl

Cutting Glass - used describing very cold weather referring to nipples getting hard

Daisy-Dukes - Extremely tight, short-shorts worn by young women in the American South

Deeferdee - D for D. Dressed for Drinks. A state of dress for woman and/or when a woman is dressed rather sluttily for a night on the town

Delete Yourself - To go away or leave

Dessert Pocket - Humorously used to refer to that part of the stomach reserved for dessert

Deuce-and-a-quarter - Reflects the number 225

Did you get my invitation - Refers to a pending invitation to bite one's lower posterior in response to a perceived insult or as a childish retort

Doink - Someone is lacking sufficient cranial capacity. A moron, idiot and etc.

Dosh - dollars + cash = dosh

Double Bagger - A member of the opposite sex with an attractive body but a face so ugly that one should put a bag over one's own head just in case the bag on the other person's head should fall off

Dribble Doll and/or Sloppy Sally - Girls who squat rather than sit on a public toilet and urinate all over the seat

Dribble Dude - Men who are incapable of hitting the yawning hole of a urinal and/or Men who don't shake off the last drop well enough

Drupple - The puddle of drool that you wake up with when you fall asleep at school or work

Duck-turd - Slang for a cigar

Dumpster Diver - Someone who looks around in dumpsters for hidden treasure

Ego fodder - Young ladies who attend singles events in the hope of meeting rich men

Elefeint - To pretend to try to stop the elevator door from closing as someone is rushing to get on

Emo - soft core punk genre and the teen fans of this

Equidelirium - A balanced state between delirium and sanity. A tightrope the common man is walking on but is conditioned to a point of oblivion

Esso assho' - The person who drives through a gas station to make a turn in order to avoid waiting her turn at a busy intersection

Express-hole - The jerk who tries to sneak in more than 10 items on the supermarket express-line

Extra Napkins - Something so good that you need extra napkins to clean up your drool

Ex-Wifeosaurous - A former female spouse

Eye Candy - A gorgeous guy, not necessarily with the intelligence to match, who you just can't take your eyes off of

Fab-Flippin-Tastic - Something that is incredibly good, so saying its' fantastic isn't enough, you have to combine three words to express your joy!

Fairy-Dust - Something too technical or obscure to understand. Probably not even worth understanding

Fank You - Blend of thank you and f*** you. Used best when talking to those you really couldn't care less about

Fat to the fifth - obese, stupid, lazy, bad smelling, and irate

Firkytoodle – Foreplay

Five Across the Face - a slap across the face

Flabam - The taking down of someone's pants with a quick swipe of the hand in an s like motion

Flip a Bitch - Make a U-turn and/or to suddenly and without warning freak out to the point where spectators might call an exorcist

Flipping a Risky - to make an illegal U-turn in a high-traffic, highly visible city street

Flirtationship - long time flirting with someone and never having any physical contact with that person

Floss - show how much money you have

Flugs - Flying hugs, for when you are in a hurry or far far away

Fo' shizzle - certainly

Frenemy - someone who is a friend but also sometimes hurts your feelings

Friend - people you communicate with on a social networking website

Frontass - a girl's gut

Frostback - A Canadian working in the USA

Fugazy - When something or someone is a fake

Funch - To flip your pillow over in the middle of the night to reveal the cold side

Fungry - A conglomerate of f***ing and hungry and/or Fungry is an extreme form of hunger; usually the result of skipping breakfast and sitting through a three hour class or meeting

Fwang - Unpleasant odor, usually associated with a person or food item

Fwinsies - The freezing winds that are let into your warm bed by other persons when they move without taking precautions to look after your warmth

Garage Time - Used to describe the time guys spend single after a breakup

Gastroporn - Food, particularly desserts that are so good they are like sin in a dish

Genetic Cul de Sac - A place showing signs of inbreeding

Get Red - Variant of redass and/or case of the ass

Ghetto Booty - Your closest buddies

Gimpner - A score of ten or more on any individual hole in golf

Gino - To screw someone, to cheat, to lie, to generally be a sleaze

Girdle - A circle of girls found in malls and high school halls, usually obstructing passage

Gloush - the action of getting soaked by a passing car hitting a large puddle

Gonna Hump That - to like something immensely

Goodfromfar - A person, usually of the opposite sex, who looks attractive at a distance, but appears much less appealing close-up

Grape smuggler - A small bikini, thong, or speedo like swimsuit worn by an older, balding, hairy male

Green-neck, Greenneck - Redneck hater

Grenade - A less attractive girl on whom one has to throw one's wingman to prevent her from exploding one's good time with her hot friend

Groundation - Being Grounded or Restricted

grr - Someone is very sexy or did something very sexy

Gummedovers - The little bits of food that get stuck between your teeth that you spend long periods of time to work out with your tongue only to chew them thoroughly...again...before swallowing them

Hatchin' jacket - Maternity dress

He-hooters - Large male breasts, resembling those of a woman. Also known as man-boobs

Heavy metal sport - Any sport being played while intoxicated and with the wrong equipment

Hedon - International unit of measurement for fun, on a scale of 1 to 100

Heebatow - Similar to shushing and/or a nice, confusing way of telling someone to be quiet

Heek - A belly button piercing

High-beams - The state of one's nipples when they are erect

Hissy Fit - to throw a fit in a particularly whiny fashion

Honey-Dew - Projects or works that are brought on, directly or indirectly, from a spouse or significant other

Hoopy-dingy - A lady's rear end

Hope n' scope - The walk around the bar checking on and hitting on anything that moves

Hoppersquash - Things that hit your windshield and stick as you are driving down the road

Hornery - It's a cross between horny and ornery

Huggle - Combination of a hug and a cuddle. More intimate than simply a hug, but more physical than a cuddle

Hugglesquash - A hug and cuddle wrapped in a tight squeeze

Hump his/her/its leg - a term used to express sexual desire towards another person

Hunky dory day - The day exactly one month after your actual birthday and this is usually celebrated when one's actual birthday has been inadvertently missed, and therefore calls for much more rigorous partying

Husblink - A husband who is here now, but don't blink or he will be gone

I'm doin' cartwheels - used when you are expected to be excited but you could care less

I'm gone - A more casual way of saying I'm leaving now

Idiot Sandwich - a gathering or a meeting of fools sitting together having a stupid discussion

Ignoranus - Someone who is both ignorant and an asshole

Inhale - To eat something with great speed and vigor, and without any conscious awareness

Ippidy - Cool, awesome

Iron-box - Slang for a virgin

Ishi - A nauseatingly ugly garment, usually in some combination of light tan, gold, red, or brown

Jabber - To talk endlessly about nothing

Jackassery - Acting like a complete jackass

Jiggerypokery - Jiggerypokery is when you are trying to insert something into a hole or something and you have to kind of tweak it to get it to fit. It never works the same way twice

Jinky - Expression of surprise--like wow, geez, dang

Jockfrost - Condition brought about from driving with a cold drink between your legs. Results in one very chilly nether area

John Deere - To cut someone's grass, steal someone's girlfriend

Jubblies - Beautifully rounded breasts. Not perfect or fantastic, but nice

Juice-chicken - A term of affection for a spouse or significant other

Juiced - Extremely built or muscular, often through the use of steroids

Jump the shark - to peak and then go down again

Junk in the trunk - A large bottom, especially when the person attached otherwise attractive

Kicked him or her to the curb - To break-off a relationship with someone, usually implying that you lived together

Kilostupid - A unit of measurement used to measure utterly moronic actions

Kinkalicious - Kinky, but also implying that the object looks good enough to eat and would taste delicious

Kinked - Referring to a sexual situation or conversation; used to express feelings of how the topic is kinky

Kisseltoe - Combination of mistletoe and kissing--the whole purpose of mistletoe

Klingons - Disgustingly lovey-dovey sweethearts, the kind who fawn over each other in public

Knick Knocks - Female's underpants
Knock Boots - To have sexual intercourse
Label Whore - A label whore is someone who only wears brand name clothes, with the name of the brand usually placed somewhere for all to see
Lack-a-Nookie - No sex for a long time
Lazy ketchup - The ketchup in restaurants that is hesitant to leave its bottle
Leg Fingers – Toes
Lick Tide - The residual moisture left on one's face after an extremely wet, more like sloppy, kiss
Linner - A meal between lunch and dinner
Linsey - A beautiful girl you can't go out with because she is related to you
Lizard King - Someone who has great power and influence, yet has the personality of a dead rodent
Looky Lou - Someone who nosey, who looks in to see what you are doing. Always looking over people's shoulders
Lowdriff - Area of body between the midriff and the pubes
Lunger - Large wad of spit
Lunner - The meal eaten in midafternoon that is a combination of a late lunch and an early dinner
Lurve - When you don't love someone because you can't or you like them way beyond like
Maal - Seductive, sexy babe....in pathetic clothes, so not chic
Mackin - making out with
Make-want - To act or behave in such a way as to cause another person (potential sex partner) to desire you
Mall Rat - Anyone who dresses as gothy as possible and wanders around malls annoying shoppers by escalators
Mandex - Spandex pants or shorts designed to be worn by men, usually constricting in the crotch area
Manwich - an odd substance that drips out of your shorts after or during sports activity

Mash Up - Taking elements from different types of music and mix them together with a new song which results in an all-new song.

Masshole - Person from Massachusetts who, by definition, is bad-tempered, in a bad mood at all times, and extremely rude

Milf - A hot woman, a female who is pleasing to the eye

Mizworm - A particularly unpleasant person--short for miserable worm

Mock-eyed - To drink alcoholic beverages to the point where you can no longer see

Monosexual - A man whose wife on becoming pregnant during their first union is refused sex forever

Moobs - Man-boobs

Moon the dog - To let your hair down, to get a little wild, to break out of a boring monotonous life

Munchking around - to do something cute, or to act cute

Munter Hunter - A person who goes for less-than-attractive people

Muzzy - Mentally fuzzy or foggy, as with sleep or drugs--unable to think straight

Nada Lotta - A whole lot of nothing

Nake - Wearing almost no clothing, to be sparsely clothed

Navel-fluff - The lint that collects within the belly-button cavity

Nearn - A dork, someone you think can't get a clue, dimwit

Neck drapery - Used to describe the layer of fatty tissue built up under the jaw--synonymous with double-chin or wattle

Nertz - The tiny slivers of rubber left on paper after erasing

Neuticle - Term used for a prosthetic testicle

Nibling - Gender-neutral term for niece or nephew

Nigglywiggly - The little paper tag hanging out of the top of a Hershey's Kiss

Nimrod - another way of telling someone they are an idiot

Nipplage - When nipples are visible through clothing because they are cold

Nipplitis - getting so cold your nipples stand on end

Noogie - When you make a fist and rub it in someone's hair

Nutter - a person that is crazy

Nutters - tight-ass pants or shorts on a male individual

Oblication - a vacation that you are obligated to go on

Obvi - obviously

Off The Chain - The bomb

Onion ass - An ass so nice it makes you want to cry

Onions - A slang term for breasts, as onions come in a variety of colors and sizes, as do breasts

Ooblydoo - A poke in the stomach (usually of an overweight person)

Oogies - The small, floaty things left behind when you allow a small child to take a sip of your drink

Oxygen thief - An utterly worthless person, without redeeming qualities of any kind

Pathete - Someone who has raised pathetic to an artform

Party head - A girl that you would get head from, if you could claim you were drunk

Peach - cute in a very special way

Peachy Turtle - Used to replace hot, cute, the bomb--the best in all categories, of a person

Peeps - closest friends or family

Petuny - Small girl, word was born from an attempt at trying to say the words petite and puny at the same time

Phuff - To blow on hot food to cool it down before you eat it

Physicality - Physical interactions with a significant other-- kissing, cuddling, etc.

Plamf - A guy who puts another person's underwear on his head and inhales

Plumber's Crack - The term used to describe someone's ass-crack showing above his pants, usually when bending down

Pocket Pool - subtle rearrangement of male parts in a public place

Ponies - Six ounce bottles of beer

Poochy - A small, but protruding belly and/or when a skinny person gets temporarily fat

Pop a cod - To burst a testicle in a nasty crash

Pop-a-squat - Have a seat, usually on the ground or floor

Pound it out - To engage in sexual relations

Pouf - A hairdo in which a large mountain of hair is piled on the crown of the head

PowerTrippin - when you tell someone exactly what you want and take control.

Prairie-doggin' - You work in a large office, open except for dividers separating work spaces. Somebody drops something or screams...and several people stand so they can pop their heads up over the partition to see what's happenin' and/or when you're desperate for a bathroom for defecation

Prawn - A girl with a great body but an ugly head. Used because with a prawn, or shrimp, you throw away the head and keep the body

Preekend - Any day of the week in which you start your weekend partying activities, in preparation for the weekend

Prettiful - Better than pretty, not quite beautiful

Princess - What your boyfriend sarcastically calls you when he's annoyed with you

Prissy - Perfect, beautiful, nothing out of place--an anti-compliment

Proximate - you are called this when your best friend gives you the 'go' to date his ex

Psshhh - Used as a response to a statement that is either derogatory or doesn't have to be said. Similar to 'Whatever'

Pudgebucket - An obese child and/or a child who is exceptionally overweight due to excessive consumption of unhealthy foods and lack of exercise

Pull a Huey - To make a U-turn while driving, especially in places where U-turns are expressly forbidden or just not appropriate

Puss-Pup - A cheese filled hotdog

Pussy-footing - To delicately and carefully (like a stalking cat) talk your way around a subject that may be controversial, or difficult to discuss

Quarterwit - Someone who is less intelligent that a halfwit

Quasimodo - To walk with an extreme limp

Queef - Something that squirts out, usually a bit nasty

Queen Bean - Someone who is very pale and fat

Rat Bastard - Someone who's being a jerk, implies that they are lower than the bastard child of a rat

Rat's ass - Amazingly ugly, resembling a train wreck only worse and/or to show severe annoyance and/or I don't care

Razbelly - The act of blowing with your mouth on a child's stomach to make a flatulent raspberry sound

Redheaded stepchild - To even be considered a redheaded stepchild you must have annoyed someone terribly or will not stop misbehaving

Red Neck Disorder - symptoms: the family tree doesn't branch

Regifting - Taking a present you don't like and giving it as a gift to someone else

Retard-Proof - Idiot proof. For something so easy that no one of average intelligence can possibly screw it up

Ridonkulous - beyond being ridiculous

Robbery - The act of stealing another male's most recent female conquest

Rock - manifests greatness

Rodee - Unsuccessful attempt to make a pass or to pick someone up

Runway Bioch - A stuck-up, snotty girl who thinks she is it

Sassy tuna - someone who is being exceptionally flirty, jaunty, or stylish

Sausage Party - A social gathering where the ratio of men to women is extremely high

Scenewhore - A person, generally a female, who you find to be at most social gatherings, usually just sitting around

Schmear - The amount of mayo and or mustard the deli puts on your sandwich

Scooby Doos - good shoes

Screwed-up-pinky Sindrome - Syndrome where the pinky finger protrudes from the hand at a 45 degree angle

Scuzbucket - Derisive term for appearance or attitude

Sea Monster - Drunk girl that sits at the bar and talks smack about other girls

Selling Tickets - to tell a lie

Senior Moment - An exhibit of behavior that would typically be associated with growing older example; forgetting your own phone number or what you were talking about in the middle of a sentence

Senseslut - Someone who is open to any and all experiences, and enjoys each one thoroughly

Sexile - To force your roommate to leave so you can have annoying, noisy sex

Shim - Replaces the use of those tedious slash words used to indicate the subject or object of a sentence: he/she and him/her. Can also be used in the possessive as in his/her

Shin Din - A party where you have lots of fun

Short Sheet - Leaving exactly two squares of the toilet paper and not replacing it with a new roll

Shotgun Wedding - Usually a marriage when the bride is pregnant--under threat and/or a forced marriage

Shut it down - Shut up. To tell a person or group of people to be quiet

Sick - extremely cool and/or possessing exceptional talent

Sideass - when a girl has lovehandles

Sideburns - what a woman has when she puts on a swimsuit but hasn't been properly shaven or waxed

Sidewalk Sale - The collection of people hanging outside a club after it closes, hoping to get a date to finish off their evening

Skank - Dirty, nasty-looking woman--haven't had a shower forever

Skanktopotomus - A fat hooker

Skinny Minny - A person who is lanky, skinny, doesn't eat very much-- often used sarcastically

Slap-Nuts - A derogatory term used to insult someone

Sleaze-train - A group of all males or all females who go out with the express aim of picking up...passengers

Smidgen - a very small amount; similar to a dab

Smush - To engage in sexual relations

Snog - Kiss

Snoozapalooza - A very boring event

Soma Number - Straight Outta My Ass Number and/or not even an estimate

Sorostitute - a physically attractive female, who looks as if she may belong to a sorority, while at the same time being dressed like a complete slut and/or a true sorostitute would wear a low-cut halter top and a short, tight skirt in the middle of wintertime

Soul patch - a tiny patch of a beard under a guy's lower lip and the rest of his face has been shaved

Spiffy - A word used to show approval or happiness in regards to something

Splattermouth - Someone that frequently splatters water out of her mouth

Stink eye - The look you get from someone who is very annoyed with you

Summer Teeth - missing teeth and/or summer here and summer there

Swampass - The disgusting condition that occurs when sitting and sweating for long periods of time

Sweatermeat – Breasts

Swim upstream - to travel a long distance to meet with a girlfriend/boyfriend, inspired by the lengths salmon go to mate

Talk smack - belittle someone

Talkin' out my mouth again - talking without thinking what you are saying and/or saying something stupid and/or putting foo Talking out my ass - not really knowing about what you're talking about, but talking about it anyway and trying to sound like you know exactly what you are in fact talking about in mouth

Tattooed out - covered with tattoos

Ten Ten - an informal meeting with management...ten minutes for you ten minutes for me

Tender - A very attractive female

That Dog'll hunt - A commonly used redneck expression to inform other rednecks that something is acceptable or will work

The Bomb - the ultimate favorite of anything

Thought-Knot - A state of extreme mental confusion

Thwedgie - the kind of wedgie you get when you are wearing a thong

Tight - fantastic

Tits - Adjective used to describe satisfaction with something; sometimes said with a thumbs-up

Toc-tic - The sound of time running backwards

Toe jam - a vile and unsightly accumulation of sock lint and toe sweat, found most predominantly in male locker rooms throughout the world

To go nookleer - to explode

Tongue-deaf - a term to describe someone who absolutely, positively cannot whistle a note

Tornado Bait - Synonym for white trash, trailer trash, redneck, cracker, etc.

Totes – totally

Touchhole - Sneaky way to call someone a touchy asshole

Touk - Another name for a ski cap

Tramp Stamp - tattoo on the lower back of a woman which is specifically placed there to be seen when wearing low riding jeans or super short shorts

Two-bagger - Someone who is so ugly that during sex you have to wear a bag on your head, too, just in case hers falls off

Two-fisted - Very drunk and holding a drink in each hand

Uffle Dust - the fluff you find after emptying your pants pockets

Uglet - Someone who is sexually unattractive to both sexes

Umfriend - Someone you're sleeping with who isn't your girlfriend, boyfriend, or significant other

Urglyburglies - That feeling in your stomach when you don't know if you're anxious or hungry or what

Upper Topper Flopper Stopper - A device worn by women to prevent their breasts from sagging

Vagenda - The catalogue of expectations a woman has of a man

Vanilla - Plain, boring, lacking excitement

Variant - When the thong rises above the pant line over the hip

Vertically challenged - a short person

Vibe - To be attracted to another person

Viewie - A very attractive girl who is present, a viewable female, pleasing to the eye

Vittle - Visible thong line. Vittle for short. A heads-up to look at someone's rear

Vixen - a hot fox, referring to an attractive female that may do harm

Vlog - web log of video entries

Vurp - Vomit-burp, that special burp accompanied by a meal or last night's beverages

Wackjob - Someone who is so stupid, annoying, or just plain retarded she might as well be whacked by a hitman to put her out of her misery

Webisode - a short video that is viewed only on-line

Weenie - like a loser but less harsh

Weeze - To take something from another without permission

What's-his-face - used for one whose name you either cannot remember and/or do not want to

Whipped - To be completely controlled by someone else

Whizzy - Something fancy, with all the bells and whistles

Who-ha - The kind of girl you don't take home to mother

Whomps - Sucks. In case parents or teachers get offended by sucks

Whoopty-do - Sarcastic form of yah or wow

Wikidemia - a term paper, which was researched only on Wikipedia.org

Witch's tit - It's an old wives' tale that the mammary gland of a female, magic-practicing individual can be used to gauge cold temperatures. Cold as a witch's tit means freezing or slightly above freezing. Any temperature below freezing is colder than a witch's tit

Womenopause - The loss of male sexual drive and function later in life

Woo-ee diaper - Really dirty diapers that make you say, Woo-ee!

Work the biscuit - This phrase was originally used in the context of a guy hitting on a girl or vice-versa. Since its conception, however, the phrase has been extended to include many other forms of action not necessarily related to dating rituals.

Would you like some cheese - A snappy retort to be used against someone who keeps interrupting in an annoying way?

Wounded Soldier - A partially-finished can or bottle of beer that can still be consumed

Xeep - Sheep--a term used to describe someone who likes to follow and imitate others

Xyz - examine your zipper

Yer Number One - Short for f*** you and/or can be accompanied with the middle finger

Yippies - Young women who find it necessary to scream each other's names at high decibels--repeatedly

Your other left - You say it when someone goes to the right, after you tell them to go left

Yuppie gunfight - when two or more people reach for their cell phone when one rings

Zippy - Okay or perfect, and/or Quick or fast

Zircon - A girl that's pretty enough to date but you can't get serious about, as in worthy of a cubic zirconia but not a diamond

Zowie - What you say when you hit your thumb with a hammer really hard

Common Text-Based Emoticons and Similes

Icon	Meaning
"Letter A"	
O(<>'<>)O	Aang
==(:-)=	Abraham Lincoln
=|:)>	Abraham Lincoln
=|:-)	Abraham Lincoln
(%-w)	Abnormal
:%)	Accountant
?:^[]	Ace Ventura
:%)%	Acne
8-[	Afraid
(ap)	Airplane
-|--'	Airplane
:-o	Alarmed
c|B-)	Ali G
(.V.)	Alien
(.V.)	Alien
(8>/--<	Alien

```
    (.)(.)
      ‾
OOOOOO      Alien
    . .
     \ /
     ‾‾‾
     / \
    \^ ^/
\^/         Alien
(<>..<>)    Alien
::-)        Alien
'.'         Alien
>(::O>      Alien
>-)         Alien
<0>..<0>    Alien
>*^,^,^~~~  Alligator
=)          Angel
^j^         Angel
O:)         Angel
(a)         Angel
O:-)        Angel
O-)         Angel
0-)<        Angel
0;)         Angel
0:)         Angel
0*-)        Angel
():)        Angel
J^          Angel
O*-)        Angel
0=)         Angel
O8-)        Angel with glasses
:-||        Angry
b (         Angry
:(          Angry
>-(         Angry
```

142

D<	**Angry**
>:(	**Angry**
>:-(	**Angry**
-_-+	**Angry**
:-Z	**Angry**
:-t	**Angry**
X-(	**Angry**
X(	**Angry**
:-@	**Angry**
:-{{	**Angry Very**
^w^	**Anime Smile**
-_-;	**Anime Sweat Drop**
_\'	**Anime Sweat Drop**
^^;	**Anime Sweat Drop**
-_-;	**Anime Sweat Drop**
(o_o)	**Annoyed**
(-_-*)	**Annoyed**
@_@	**Annoyed**
¬¬	**Annoyed**
>_<*	**Annoyed**
:/	**Annoyed**
>:-(	**Annoyed**
(¬_¬")	**Annoyed**
-o,,o,,o'	**Ant**
>: o	**Antelope**
<--I-->	**Anyway**
8-[	**Anxious**
m(_)m	**Apology**
＼(_ _)	**Apology**
m(T-T)m	**Apology**
=D>	**Applause**
(^^)//	**Applause**
0-+	**April**
>A<	**Archangel**
<')))~	**Armadillo**

,,\(o3o)/,,	**Armpit Hair**
>--->>	**Arrow**
<---<<<	**Arrow**
<|-)	**Asian**
:-Y	**Aside Comment**
<:-)	**Ask a dumb question**
|-|	**Asleep**
|I	**Asleep**
:C	**Astonished**
:-C	**Astonished**
8-O	**Astonished**
(0)-<-<	**Astronaut**
@==	**Atom bomb**
~X(	**At Wits End**
X:-)	**Aunt Jemima**
(au)	**Auto**
:S	**Awkward**

"Letter B"

:=8)	**Baboon**
~:0	**Baby**
~O><	**Baby**
[{-_-}]	**Baby**
][	**Back-to-Back**
d:- \	**Bad Boy**
~~8-O	**Bad-Hair Day**
(8-)	**Bald**
C:-|	**Bald**
:-)-S=~	**Ballerina**
o~	**Balloon**
((	**Banana**
(::()::)	**Band-Aid**
(::[]::)	**Band-Aid**
(:::X:::)	**Band-Aid**
:▶	**Bandit**

~'v	**Bangs**
:-%	**Banker**
:-C~	**Barfing**
8o|	**Baring Teeth**
:-E	**Baring Teeth**

```
^^^^^^^
   |   |
  | O  O|
  c ,___|
    | ]
```

	Bart Simpson
d:-)	**Baseball Player**
d:-p	**Baseball Player**
q:-)	**Baseball Player**
d:)	**Baseball Player**
:-)	**Basic**
:-{0	**Basic Mustache**
^v^	**Bat**
(^+.+^)	**Bat**
B-|	**Batman**
;;)	**Batting Eyelashes**
:~-(	**Bawling**
(")-.-(")	**Bear**
\'''\(*.*)/'''/	**Bear**
:-){	**Beard**
(:-{~	**Beard – long**
%+{	**Beat-Up**
: =	**Beaver**
( )	
:(III)-	**Bee**
( )	
~(,)~	**Bee**
:bz	**Bee**
%-|	**Been up All Night**
[%]D	**Beer Mug**
m(-_-)m	**Begging**

::::[||]::::	Belt
&:-o-8-<	Betty Boop
#:o+=	Betty Boop
o_0	Bewildered
~ __0	
_-\<,_	Bicycle
(*)/ (*)	
(*)/ (*)	Bicycle
--==Ⓧh\Ⓧ	Bicycle
:-)^<	Big Boy
(:-)	Big Face
:-)8<	Big Girl
:->	Big grin happy
D	Big Grin
:-D	Big Grin
>:D<	Big Hug
(((H)))	Big Hug
8|___)	Big Laugh
:-(|)	Big Lips
(|X0||)	Big Mac
<(:?)	Big-Nosed Dunce
*|:^)(.)(…)	Big Snowman
:-X	Big Wet Kiss
=|:o}	Bill Clinton smiley
(*v*)	Bird
~:<>	Bird
(^)	Birthday Cake
*<:)	Birthday Hat
<>:-)	Bishop
:*x	Biting
:-s	Bizarre Comment
(:-D	Blabber Mouth
?(	Black Eye
?-(	Black Eye
;-(	Black Eye Angry

'8^P	Blah
(:-	Blank Expression
|-(	Blind
#-)	Blinking
^^	Blissful
:c)	Blissful
:-]	Blockhead
:-{}	Blowing a Kiss
Э(°O°)Є	Blowfish
*8=(:	Blubbering
:-*>	Blushing
:*-)	Blushing
:-">	Blushing
:,')	Blushing
=">	Blushing
=^}	Blushing
:")	Blushing
=^_^=	Blushing
=<_<=	Blushing
@=	Bomb
:/	Bored
(-_-)	Bored
\-o	Bored
:-o zz	Bored
:-o	Bored
:|	Bored
I:(	Botox smiley
(/-_·)/D····>	Bow and Arrow
m(_ _)m	Bowing
(||)	Bowl
===O____iii	Bowling
___O___III	Bowling
____o/|||	Bowling
:-}X	Bow Tie
:-)8	Bow Tie

o(^_-)O	Boxer
Q("q) Q("Q)	Boxing
(z)	Boy
(:-)	Boy
:-)^<	Boy
:-#	Braces
:-{#}	Braces
=#	Braces
%-6	Brain Dead
[<O>]	Brazilian Flag
(o)(o)	Breasts (Boobs)
>:/	Bring it On
%-(	Broken Glasses
(U)	Broken Heart
=((	Broken Heart
(u)	Broken Heart
<\3	Broken Heart
</3	Broken Heart
<~3	Broken Heart
:^)	Broken nose
:-(=)	Bucktoothed
:-E	Bucktoothed Vampire
:-F	Bucktoothed vampire w/ One Tooth Missing
}|{	Bug
=:)	Bug
0_0	Bug
E=B	Bugs Bunny
pq`#'	Bull
):|	Bull
[O==O\=<(	Bulldozer
=;-(	Bully
00	
('.')	Bunny
(")(")	

(_/)
(o.o)   Bunny
(___)0
(=^_^=)   Bunny
(O:3   Bunny
(_/)   Bunny Ears
#-(Bureaucrat
:-#| Bushy Mustache
:-)</////>   Businessman
(|_)   Butt
(_!_)   Butt
}|{   Butterfly
})i({   Butterfly
}i{   Butterfly
})U({   Butterfly
ƎӜЗ   Butterfly

"Letter C"

```
      ,,,,,
     _|||||_
    {~*~*~*~}      Cake
   _{*~*~*~*}_
    `----------`
```

>(///)<   Candy
P=\\   Cap
((-_(-_-)_-))   Care Crowd
❀[{O{]_+-_]❀ Casket
}:-X   Cat
=^.^=   Cat
q:-)   Catcher
(:@@@@@D Caterpillar
>^..^<   Cat Face
^-.-^ Zzzzz   Cat Nap
~o(:-)   Cave Diver
(<._.>)   Charlie Brown

149

|-{	**Charlie Brown**
C|:-=	**Charlie Chaplin**
:-@	**Chatterbox**
\o/	**Cheer**
\O/	**Cheerleader**
C=:-)	**Chef**
(:=3	**Chef**
~:>	**Chicken**
<°)	**Chicken**
(*>	**Chicken**
C8o)	**Chimp**
C8o (	**Chimp**
C8o \	**Chimp**
-{:-]	**Chinese Hat**
;-(	**Chin up**
\)))/ & \~~~/	**Chips and Dip**
*<<<<+	**Christmas tree**

```
  X
  /\
 /. \          Christmas Tree
/__\
 |_|
```

<{^-^}>	**Chubby Face**
:-.)	**Cindy Crawford**
(:)	**Clam**
(o)	**Clock**
<]:o){	**Clown**
*:o)	**Clown**
<|:^0|<	**Clown**
*<:o)	**Clown**
*<:^)	**Clown**
*<:oP	**Clown**
*<:oB	**Clown**
(c:>*	**Clown**
*<8-)X	**Clown**

><*:oDX	Clown
:O)	Clown
*<):o)	Clown
:*)	Clowning
=:-)	Cobbler
(c)	Coffee Cup
:~)	Cold
:-{}	Cold
:-~|	Cold and/or Flu
?_?	Cold Stare
$:-)	Comb Stuck in the Hair
@/:^)	Conan
:-r	Concentrating
:-8(	Condescending Stare
:-Q	Confused
:-/	Confused
:-S	Confused
:s	Confused
:-$	Confused
(@_@)	Confused
=?	Confused
,':(	Confused
:-??	Confused
(p_q)	Confused
‾\(°_o)/‾	Confused
:~/	Confused
%)	Confused
O.o	Confused
%-(	Confused
:-S	Confused
:s	Confused
@@@	Cookies
B-)	Cool
qB-)	Cool
Ж-D	Cool

(-}{-)	Couple kissing
3:o	Cow
+/"\	Cowbell
<):-)	Cowboy
}:-)	Cowboy
<):)	Cowboy
C):)	Cowboy
(-:(3	Cowboy
{:-)	Cowgirl
▤)O{)д|><	Cowgirl
V.v.V	Crab
V.^.V	
( )	Crab
[[ ]]	
(∨)!_!(∨)	Crab
()_RED_(>	Crayon
())Crayola))>	Crayon
%-)	Crazy
>,=,-	Crocodile
H-)	Cross-Eyed
>.<	Cross-Eyed
:_(	Crying
T_T	Crying
:'(	Crying
;_;	Crying
:"-(	Crying
:`-(	Crying
:*(	Crying softly
C(_)	Cup of Coffee
[_]>	Cup of coffee
_P	Cup of Coffee
_/?	Cup of tea
&:-)	Curly Hair
:-@!	Cursing
n_n	Cute

@-|	Cyborg
o-)	Cyclops
O-(	Cyclops
.)	Cyclops
Q-)	Cyclops
*-(	Cyclops
"Letter D"	
:)-S=	Dancer
\:D/	Dancing
^(. .)^	Dancing
<(..<)	Dancing
(>..)>	Dancing
~(o.o)~	Dancing
\(^o\) (/o^)/	Dancing
v(*.*)^	Dancing
C8<]	Darth Vader
/oo\	Darth Vader
Q:|	Davey Crockett
8->	Daydreaming
-	Dazed
x_x	Dead
8-#	Dead
(X_X)	Dead
(°)	Death Star
x.x	Dead
XP	Dead
3:*)	Deer
—(T_T)->	Defeated
:-| :-|	Deja Vu
._.	Depressed
(<_>)	Depressed
:-[	Despondent
i-)	Detective
>:)	Devil

(6)	Devil
]:->	Devil
}:-)	Devil
(){}:o)	Devil
}=^{|~	Devil
3:)	Devil
>:-)~	Devil
>;->	Devil
]:-)	Devil – Happy
>:-)	Devil – Happy
>-)	Devil Wink
>->	Devil Wink
>:->	Diabolical
{>O	Diamond Ring
:-')	Dimple
*<	
[<	Dinosaur
/\	
=|:-)X	Diplomat
:-e	Disappointed
:e	Disappointed
:-|	Disappointed
:|	Disappointed
:(&	Disappointed
=\	Disappointed
‾‿‾)	Discontent
DX	Disgusted
:§‾‾	Disgusted
(*‾m‾)	Dissatisfied
/:(	Distraught
%-}	Dizzy
d[-_-]b	DJ
[:-}	DJ
d^_^b	DJ
:-)-o	Doctor

O:v)>--o	Doctor
:3-]	Dog
O\'	Dog
:O?	Dog
:O/	Dog
:O$	Dog
:O)	Dog
<[.,=.,]-	Dog
<[~.~]>	Dog
:o3	Dog
8==3	Dog Bone
&===3	Dog bone
(&)	Dog Face
(>.<)	Doh
#-o	Doh!
[(1)]	Dollar
(y):-p	Donald Trump
:-$	Do Not Tell Anyone
:-#	Do Not Tell Anyone
(o)	Donut
(8)<=	Doraemon
:D))	Double Chin
: T	Doubtful
12x@>--->---	Dozen Roses
}:-(=	Dracula
(>:^F)	Dracula
^.=.^	Dragon
I-)	Dreaming
:*)	Drinking every night
:)_	Drooling
=P~	Drooling
:-P	Drooling
:P	Drooling
:-B	Drooling
(*¬*)	Drooling

:#)	**Drunk**
%*}	**Drunk**
:*)	**Drunk**
:*)?	**Drunk**
%-<I>	**Drunk**
|__(o)>	**Duck**
(`_)?(_')	**Dueling**
:-F	**Dufus**
:|	**Dull**
p^b	**Dumb**
8)	**Dumb Person**
<:-l	**Dunce**
<:-(	**Dunce**

"Letter E"

:-6	**Eating Something Spicy**
(:-|	**Egghead**
ε= ┌(≧▽)┘	**Elated**
~~\8-O	**Electrocuted**
\/\/\/\,8-O	**Electrocuted**
:~	**Elephant**
~:3	**Elephant**
@(' ')@ \/	**Elephant**
*<:-)	**Elf**
5:-)	**Elvis**
~:-\	**Elvis**
~:\	**Elvis**
:-$	**Embarrassed**
:$	**Embarrassed**
:-[	**Embarrassed**
^^"	**Embarrassed**
:-}	**Embarrassed Smile**
//_^	**Emo**
(//_^)	**Emo**

(//.^)	Emo
(//_-)	Emo
c//_+.	Emo
c//_^'	Emo
c/_-*	Emo
(-_\\\)	Emo
//_T)o.	Emo
d(//^)b	Emo
0|-)	Enjoying the Sun
(@){	Euphonium
>:)	Evil
>:3	Evil Cuteness
(.\\|/.)	Evil Face
):D}	Evil Face
:{)	Evil Face
>:~>	Evil Face
>:{)>	Evil Face
]}:-)>	Evil Face
>-)	Evil Grin
>:)	Evil Grin
>:D	Evil Laugh
>=)	Evil Smile
/^^\!	Exasperated
:-O	Excited
(*-*)	Excited
:@	Exclamation "What???"
:-6	Exhausted
#-)	Exhausted
_|‾|o	Exhausted
}=D	Eyebrows
-@--@-	Eyeglasses
P-)	Eye Patch
b-)	Eye Patch
Q_Q	Eyes Popping Out of Head

"Letter F"

}{	Face-to-Face
(6.6)	Fainting
(ñ_ñ)	Fake Smile
(p ^^)====O	Falcon Punch
?:-)	Fancy Hair
o,..,o	Fangs
^,..,^	Fangs
===[]===	Fasten Your Seatbelt
=^O.O^=	Felix the Cat
O+	Female
O	
±	Female
^	
>-	Female
O<-<=	Female
;~[	Fighter
G(-'.'G)	Fighting Kid
(~)	Filmstrip
()))))-x	Firecracker
<><	Fish
}-(((*>	Fish
<")))><	Fish
><(((">	Fish
<.{{{><	Fish
{}{	Fish
<((((><	Fish
<('O')>	Fish
<*)))<	Fish
(~)	Fish Bowl
~==	Flame (inflammatory message)
~:-(	Flame Message
~~:-(	Flame Message – Hot
i-=<***	Flamethrower
!.'v	Flat Top

l:-O	FlatTop Loudmouth
OZ~<	Flexing
;D	Flirting
;-)	Flirty
@>---	Flower
@>--;--	Flower
<-#	Flower
0==I==,=I==	Flute
D';	FML
O-&-<	Folding Arms
:-!	Foot in Mouth
()	Football
G:-)	Football Helmet
=:-H	Football player
:-!	Foot in Mouth
:-W	Forked Tongue
|:-<	Forlorn
%%-	Four Leaf Clover
< '!' >	Fox
[:-|	Frankenstein
E:/	Frankenstein
[8-]	Frankenstein
:^{=	Frank Zappa
%*@:-)	Freaking Out
P*	French Kiss
:Pd:	French Kiss
/:-)	Frenchman with a beret
8-|	Frightened
8)~~*	Frog
<? ?>	Frog
8)	Frog
:(?)	Frog
[II]D	Frosty Mug
:-(	Frown
:(	Frown

:o{	Frown
:-(	Frowning
X[	Frustrated
><	Frustrated
B/	Frustrated
>.<*	Frustrated
-_-*	Frustrated
=P	Frustrated
}: [	Frustrated
:-P	Frustrated
:-L	Frustrated
|-[#]	Fuming
:-D	Funny
:/)	Funny, Not
>>:-<<	Furious
>-<	Furious
(ò_ó)	Furious
:	Fuzzy
:}	Fuzzy With a Mustache

"Letter G"

: 0=/--	Gag Me
:-(*)	Gag Me
qB]	Gangster
@}:-)	Gardener
=:o	Gasp
3>(	Geezer
(D:-]	General
@:i	Genie
{@:)}	Genie
4:-)	George Washington
~~:-(	Getting Rained On
d=P	Ghetto
(>")>	Ghost
<(")>	Ghost

(",)	Ghost
(: (=|	Ghost
8[+]	Gift
;))	Giggle
^ ^ ^	Giggles
>:o===Q<	Giraffe
(x)	Girl
8:^)	Girl
(-_-)#	Girl
~0(**)0~	Girl
((((Person))))	Giving them a virtual hug
>:[	Glaring
\~/	Glass
_/	Glass
\~/	Glass with a drink (Usually booze)
8-)	Glasses
??	Glasses
-o-o-	Glasses
()-()	Glasses
-@--@-	Glasses
\o-o/	Glasses
(-_q)	Glasses
8*)	Glasses and a Half Mustache
:-{>	Goatee
;€	Goatee
o/	Golf
|-{	Good Grief!
♪(●′∇`)/	Good Night
(ToT)/~~~	Goodbye
(^ _ ^)/~~	Goodbye
8]	Gorilla
%:O	Gorilla
8:]	Gorilla
(:-D	Gossip, blabbermouth
|<:-)	Graduate

L:-)	**Graduate**
Q:-)	**Graduate**
oO:)&	**Grandma**
(~};)	**Grateful Dead**
$_$	**Greedy**
(v)	**Greedy**
\o o/	**Greeting**
.'!	**Grim**
:->	**Grin**
=^D	**Grin**
:D	**Grin**
¦-D	**Grin**
:oP	**Grin**
(¯—¯)	**Grinning**
:oÞ	**Grinning and sticking tongue out**
v(*.*)^	**Grooving**
l:['	**Groucho Marx**
[>#<]	**Grouchy**
>:(	**Grumpy**
<:-(	**Grumpy**
^i^	**Guardian Angel**
>I<	**Guardian Angel**
^_^;	**Guilty**
{ o }===(:::)	**Guitar**
︻┳デ═—	**Gun**
︻╦╤─	**Gun**
╓╤╤─	**Gun**
S:~)	**Guy**
$8()	**Guy with a Toupee**

"Letter H"

*8D	Hair
((:D	Hair
~~8-O	Hair
@:-)	Hair
#:-)	Hair
~#:-(	Hair
?:-)	Hair
%-.-%	Hair
@.'v	Hair
}:-)	Hair parted
{:-{)}	Hairy
L-:	Half Smile
(|||	Hamburger
E-:-)	Ham radio operator
(%)	Handcuffs
:-})	Handlebar Mustache
(:>-<	Hands Up
:-|><	Hands Up
&:-]	Handsome
=)	Happy
:^D	Happy
:-)	Happy
:)	Happy
*<|:o)	Happy Birthday
:-0 hbtu 0-:	Happy Birthday To You
:'-)	Happy Crying
:")	Happy Tears
<~8)	Harry Potter
>O<	Harry Potter Snitch
/* *	Harry Potter Wand
:%)%	Has Acne
:-'	Has a Dimple
:(#)	Has Braces variation
q=)	Hat

163

xd:)	Hat
*<:)	Hat
+(:-)	Hat
*<.'v	Hat
d.'v	Hat
d :-o	Hat's Off
:-`|	Have a Cold
:{	Having a hard time
(({..}))	Headache
(|:-)	Headband
>:^(	Headhunter
oo	Headlights
d(-_-)b	Headphones
0(o.o)0	Headphones
[:-)	Headphones
((d[-.-]b))	Headphones
q[-'.'-]p	Headphones
:X	Hear no evil
<3	Heart
♥	Heart
<u3	Heart
S2	Heart
»-(¯`·.·´¯)->	Heart
./\..|..|....	Heart Monitor
\M/	Heavy Metal Music
/;-)	Heavy Eyebrows – Slanted
▼o·_·o▼	Hello
?:)#	Hema Employee
l^o	Hepcat
(·_·;)_·)	Hiding
^5	High Five
(h5)	High Five
o/\o	High Five
^_^/	High Five
^y^-/|\--Y^	Highway

o->	Hiro
:-\	Hmmm
:-/	Hmmm
L.	Hockey Stick
L.	Hockey Stick and Puck
8-)	Hollywood
(8-(1)	Homer
(8(|)	Homer
(_8^(1)	Homer Simpson
~(_8^(|)	Homer Simpson
(8(|)	Homer Simpson
o--}	Hope
o(^^o)(o^^)o	Hopeful
}:)	Horny
(^~^~^)	Hot Ass Walking Away
{ }	Hug
[], ()	Hug
(:)\/<	Hug
:)X	Hug
(>")><("<)	Hug
(((H)))	Hug
{*}	Hug and Kiss
<(^.^<)	Huge
<(*.*<)	Huggle
:D<	Hugs
((()))	Hugs
{{{***}}}	Hugs and Kisses
(( )):**	Hugs and Kisses
*^_^*	Huge Dazzling Grin
~!~	Humbled
%*@:-(	Hung Over
#-)	Hung Over
%-\	Hung Over
:0	Hungry
:-[]	Hungry

:!!	**Hurry Up**
-(@ @)-	**Hypnotist**
U	
@-)	**Hypnotized**

"Letter I"

o[-<]:	**I am a skater or I like to skate**
< }	**Ice Cream**
< }}	**Ice Cream**
~oO>	**Ice Cream Cone**
<OO	**Ice Cream Cone**
<Oo*	**Ice Cream Cone**
<><	**Ichthus**
*-:)	**Idea**
!:-)	**I have an idea**
::poof::	**I'm Gone**
(@)	**In a Nut Shell**
%*}	**Inebriated**
:-|	**Indifferent**
8	**Infinity**
<3+<3	**In Love**
(♥_♥)	**In Love**
7/	**Indecisive**
:-|	**Indifferent**
:-I	**Indifferent**
(*′∇ ` *)	**Infatuated**
(*°∀°)=3	**Infatuated**
0:-)	**Innocent**
§)	**Insane**
%-}	**Ironic**
?_?	**Irritated**
%7<	**Irritated**

"Letter J"

(:-|K-	James Bond
8(>_<)8	Jealous
(|):-)=II=	Jewish Blonde
(8 {	John Lennon
//o-o\\	John Lennon
((*J*))	John Lennon
X-p	Joking
:-]	Jovial
\m/<(^_^)>\m/	Joyful
(≧∇≦)/	Joyful
o(^o^)o	Joyful
@:-}	Just Back From Hairdresser
X-(	Just Died

"Letter K"

:-x	Keeping mouth shut
(:-#	Keeping Quiet
(((oo)))	Kenny-Southpark
(((xx)))	Kenny (dead) –Southpark
X:-)	Kid
\VVV/	King
\$$$/	King
]: =]===>	King Arthur
<(^.^)>	Kirby
<('.')>	Kirby
<('.'<)	Kirby
(>'.')>	Kirby
<(^_^)>	Kirby
:-)*	Kiss
:*]	Kiss
:-*	Kiss
(:-*	Kiss
:*	Kiss
:-x	Kiss

:x	Kiss
=^*	Kisses
('}{')	Kissing
(-}{-)	Kissing
(_X_)	Kiss my Butt
:-*	Kiss on the cheek
:-X	Kiss on the lips
:**:	Kiss Returned
>^,,^<	Kitty Cat - it's a straight-on smiley
>*	Kitty doesn't like taking its pill
~*=	Kitty running away from you
:p	Kitty with tongue hanging out
[|]	Kleenex
>:-l	Klingon
+<||-)	Knight
+<#^v	Knight
(^^) //('_')\\ (^^)	Knuckles
:*)O	Kool
@(*0*)@	Koala - it's a straight-on smiley
[]8)	Kyle - Southpark

"Letter L"

<{::}>	Ladybug
(::)<	Ladybug
|-D	Laugh
XD	Laughing
(^_^)	Laughing
%OD	Laughing like crazy
=D	Laughing Out Loud
:-D	Laughter
/\/\/\	Laughter
(-:	Left Handed Happy Face
)-:	Left Handed Sad Face
?-:	Left Handed Tongue Touching Nose
({)	Left Hug

>;->	Lewd Remark
:^o	Liar Liar
:-9	Licking Lips
:-?	Licking Lips
;-,	Like, Duh
:-*	Lips are Sealed
:-X	Lips are Sealed
:X	Lips are Sealed
:()	Lipstick
:-{}	Lipstick
d-_-b	Listening to Music
d^_^b	Listening to Music
d(^_^)b	Listening to Music
8:-)	Little Girl
>-<	Livid
~~I==I>	Lizard
@---	Lollipop
:P@---	Lollipop
:-----)	Long nose (Liar!)
<@> <@>	Look at Me
(*)?(*)	Looking
>_>	Looking
<_<	Looking
>.>	Looking
<.< >.>	Looking Around
<o?o>	Looking at You
<*_*>	Looking at You
>.>	Looking
L-)	Loser
%+{	Lost a Fight
|-(	Lost Contact Lenses
:-{}	Lots of Lipstick
:( )	Loudmouth
<3	Love
~♥~	Love

:x	**Love Struck**
__.	**Lying Down**

"Letter M"

(m)(m)(m)	**M&Ms**
X-(	**Mad**
>:-<	**Mad**
>:0	**Mad**
~ :-(	**Mad**
=/	**Mad**
>=(	**Mad**
>_<	**Mad**
:-.)	**Madonna**
<*:-)	**Magician**
&-l	**Makes Me Cry**
:-S	**Makes No Sense**
:-(*)	**Makes Me Sick**
O->	**Male**
8-	**Male**
:-	**Male**
0-|-[	**Man**
@@@@:-)	**Marge Simpson**
(@@@@):^)	**Marge Simpson**
######:o)	**Marge Simpson**
@@@:)	**Marge Simpson**
(#-[	**Marine**
:-)(-:	**Married**
☺ ☺ ♥	
/|\./|\ ⊥⊥	**Married**
-----(_)-	**Marshmallow**
-()_)-()_)—	**Marshmallow**
(.!.)	**Martian**
=:)	**Martian**
Q>--|	**Martini**

(d)	Martini Glass
|>--|	Martini Glass
>:-I	Mean
@|-)	Meditating
(-_-)	Meditating
O O	
/|\ /|\	Men
∧ ∧	
iiii'i'iiii	Menorah
@_@	Mesmerized
#:-)	Messy Hair
\m/	Metal
8(:-)	Mickey Mouse
|:-[|]	Mick Jagger
,,!,,	Middle Finger
:)	Midget
o/<	Midget
(o:v)	Miner
:p	Mischievous
:}	Mischievous
?8}	Mischievous
=)=	Mixed Feelings
-:-)	Mohawk
=.'v	Mohawk
[*(1)*]	Money
+<:-|	Monk
:(|)	Monkey
@(^_^)@	Monkey
(;_·)	Monocle
:E	Monster
>:(><)	Monster
(_i_)	Mooning You
(|)	Mooning You
(>°|°<)	Mosquito
<:3)~	Mouse

~O-O~	**Mr. Magoo**
:-{	**Mustache**
{:-{)}	**Mustache and Beard**
:-3	**Mustache (Handlebar Type)**
:-#	**My Lips Are Sealed**
:-X	**My Lips Are Sealed**
= X	**My Lips Are Sealed**

"Letter N"

(Z(:^P	Napoleon
~,~	Napping
_:^)	Native American
*:-)	Navy Admiral
@:-)	Navy Captain
#:-)	Navy Commander
=:-)	Navy Lieutenant
(-)	Needs Haircut
# 8 -)	Nerd and/or person w/ glasses & crew cut
:-B	Nerd
8-B	Nerd
QK	Ninja
[-_-]~	Ninja
Qx	Ninja
):-(	Nordic
{}	No Comment
<:@0	Nose
(:^(	Nose
(:+)	Nose
:/\)	Nose
:v)	Nose
>*(	Nose
.^v	Nose
%-(	Not Listening
:/I	No Smoking
:/)	Not Amused

[-(	Not talking
^:)^	Not Worthy
+<:-|	Nun
]:-)	Nurse

"Letter O"

O_o	Oddball
:-j	Oh Go On
?:-_]	Old Lady
|:-{}~	Old Man
8-O	Omigod!
:)]	On the Phone
'-)	One-Eyed Smile
°-)	One-Eyed Smile
.-)	One-Eyed Smile
>.-)	One-Eyed Smile
`:-)	One eyebrow raised
:-D	Open-Mouthed Smile
:d	Open-Mouthed Smile
E:-)	Operator
:=)	Orangutan
~#|__/~~\o/~	Overboard
^_^	Overjoyed
.^_^.	Overjoyed
:-)))	Overweight
(QvQ)	
( )	Owl
" "	
(^o^)	Owl

"Letter P"

(>_<)	Painful
\(>o<)/	Panicking
(>-:-)-<	Parachute
(@.@)	Paranoid

<:-P	Party
<:o)	Party
*<(:)	Party Hat
<l:0	Partying
*<(8)~/~<	Partying
*<|8-P~	Partying Too Much
(:V	Pato
:)>-	Peace
(/|\)	Peace
V (*_*) V	Peace
(^o^)y	Peace
<IIEEEEEED	Pen
0))__)>	Pencil
8>	Penguin
<(")	Penguin
<(^)	Penguin
:-/	Perplexed
<:^]	Person
O<-<	Person
:^)	Personality
3:]	Pet Dog
{8^(3	Peter Griffin (Family Guy)
----|}	Pie Being Thrown
--===[}	Pie Fight
(~_(|=--Z(◡ˇ)	Pie Fight
=8)	Pig
:8)	Pig
<(^oo^)>	Pig
^(*(oo)*)^	Pig
:@)	Pig smile
/***(^o^)***\	Pigtails
^_^''	Pikachu
(o^-^o)	Pikachu
<(:-)	Pilgrim
:---)	Pinocchio

:-------[	Pinocchio
P-(	Pirate
-=,q	Pistol
3:[	Pitbull
<%)	Pizza
O-G-<	Pointing
}:^#)	Pointy Nosed
-[[•]]--[()]-	Police Chase
[|:-{O	Police Officer
:-I	Pondering
~@~	Poop
[:::::]	Pop-Tart
+<:-)	Pope
+O=-)	Pope
;-?	Popeye
:-t	Pouting
>:-[	Pouting
\o/	Praise the Lord
O/	Praise the Lord
/\'s	Prayers
[-o<	Praying
:-)>( )-	Pregnant
&	Pretzel
+:-)	Priest
\<><>/	Prince
~<:-)	Princess
\&&&/	Princess
@(*-*)@	Princess Leia
x{|:)	Propeller Hat
X:-)	Propeller Head
%(|:-)	Propeller Head
?-)	Proud of black eye
>.<	Pucker face - it's a straight-on smiley
|-<>	Puckered Up to Kiss
:-><	Puckered Up to Kiss

175

(^:^)	Pumpkin
(~~)	Pumpkin
:+(	Punched in the Nose
=:-)	Punk
-:-/	Punk
=:-(	Punk Not Smiling
/(^.^)\	Puppy
Q('.'Q)	Put Em Up
:-($)	Put your money where your mouth is
:-k	Puzzlement

"Letter Q"

C):-O	
C):-O	Quartet
C):-O	
C):-O	
\%%%/	Queen

"Letter R"

>-=]	Rabbit
('.') OO	Rabbit
=(-,-)= (")_(")	Rabbit
~~:-(	Rain
`:-)	Raised Eyebrow
:-r	Raspberry
<:3( )~~	Rat
--- :	Rat
=:7)~~	Rat
=:7(~~	Rat
(((((:-{=	Rave Dude
^RUP^	Read Up Please
:-C	Real Unhappy
~:-(	Really Bummed Out

:-))	**Really Happy**
}---:o>	**Reindeer**
+<:-)	**Religious leader or person**
~o)	**Reproduction**
>=D	**Revenge**
?$?:-)	**Rich**
(})	**Right Hug**
*<l:o)>	**Robin Hood**
([(	**Robocop**
[:]	**Robot**
:|]	**Robot**
[:|]	**Robot**
<(-_-)>	**Robot**
d(>_<)b	**Rocker**
<:-)<<|	**Rocket**
\m/	**Rocking**
\m/ >_< \m/	**Rocking Out**
\m/(**)\m/	**Rock On**
\m/@_@\m/	**Rock On**
O -- [] -- ✂	**Rock, Paper, Scissors**
@@	**Rolling your eyes**
8-|	**Rolling Eyes**
>>	**Rolling Eyes**
9_9	**Rolling Eyes**
7:^)	**Ronald Reagan**
~:>	**Rooster**
@~)~~~	**Rose**
@-->---	**Rose**
--{--@	**Rose**
@};---	**Rose**
@>--;--	**Rose**
())>---	**Rose**
3:*>	**Rudolph the red nose reindeer**
== 0>--< ==	**Run Over**
┌(;•_•)┘	**Running**

$\varepsilon = \ulcorner (>\_<) \lrcorner$ Running

"Letter S"

:(	Sad
=(	Sad
(:-\	Sad
:-(	Sad with nose
:-y	Said with a Smile
:-d	Said with a smile
/:-)	Sailor
;-)}<////>	Salesman
>>>>(:-)	Salesman
m:-)	Salute
*<]:{)	Santa
*<:-)	Santa Claus
*<|:-{)}	Santa Claus
*<|:^) }	Santa Claus
<|:)}	Santa Claus
0<[]:-)>>	Santa Claus
*-={:-)}}}>	Santa Claus
*<|:o)>	Santa Claus
:-]	Sarcasm
:-7	Sarcastic
:->	Sarcastic
;s	Sarcastic
!#!^*&:-)	Schizophrenic
!:-)	Scholar
8<	Scissors
c--I-I-I{	Scorpion
:-@	Scream
:-@	Screaming
)8-)	Scuba Diver with Hair
..._[:]	Scuba Diver
..._(:)-o	Scuba Diver
m-)	See No Evil

8==8	Seeing Eye to Eye
\$__\$	Sees Money
:-i	Semi-Smile
;-)~	Sexy tongue - or drunk
\000/	Shaka
9(x.x)9	Shaking Fist
(x.x)9	Shaking Fist
<(((">	Shark
~~/\\~~~	Shark
>---^-*<	Shark
_/____\0/__	Shark
_/_\0/_	Shark Attack
C):-| *	Sheriff
8-0	Shocked
#:-o	Shocked
=O	Shocked
:-o	Shocked
+-(	Shot Between the Eyes
*-)	Shot to Death
:-V	Shouting
|----D	Shovel
‾\(°_°)/‾	Shrugging
(*^_^*)	Shy
-_-	Shy
(^^;)	Shy
(#^.^#)	Shy
(-:|:-)	Siamese Twins
%-)	Silly
~:-P	Single Hair
:O	Singing
O-\-<]:	Skateboarder
O[-<]:	Skateboarder
o<[^(	Skater
o->-</:	Skater
q=)-<--<|:	Skater

:-/	Skeptical
':-/	Skeptical again
:-7	Skeptical variation
ε= ┌(^-^)┘	Skipping
-_-	Sleeping
|-)	Sleepy
:-)	Smile
=]	Smile
>-)	Smile
O-)	Smiley after Smoking a Banana
):-)	Smiley with Hair
:-,	Smirk
;^)	Smirking
:-p~	Smoker
:-d~	Smoker
:-Q~	Smoking
:- i	Smoking a cig
:-?	Smoking a pipe
:>	Smug
@x	Snail
_@/	Snail
`@____	Snail
@_v	Snail
@_ö	Snail
~~8}	Snake
=====:}	Snake
:-\'|	Sniffles
<:-oOO	Snowman
|^O	Snoring
-=	Snuffed Candle
c]:{D	Sombrero
>.<	Sour
|-=[O]=-|	Spaceship
:-m	Speak No Evil
/\(00)/\	Spider

8\'B	Sponge Bob
[:-]	Square Head
:)	Standard smile
:-(<|	Standing Firm
=%-O	Stared at Computer Way Too Long
%-)	Staring at a Screen for 15 hours
O -|- /\	Stick Man
:P	Sticking tongue out (raspberry)
:-P	Sticking Tongue Out
:-f	Sticking Tongue Out
:-r	Sticking Tongue Out
O=[O{|__|]=O	Stretcher
@?@	Stunned
B-)	Sunglasses
(8-{)}	Sunglasses, Mustache, Beard
/8^{~	Sunglasses, Mustache, Goatee
:-<	Super sad
:o	Surprised
:-O	Surprised
>:-@!	Swearing
`:-)	Sweating
,:-)	Sweating on the Other Side
:D	Sweet, big smile for you
8-)	Swimmer
B-)-[<	Swimming Trunks
oxx:{}:::::::>	Sword
cxxx{}:::::::>	Sword
0]xxx]====>	Sword
---(|||]==[]	Syringe
+=>-	Syringe

"Letter T"

:-0	**Talkative**
:-{ }	**Talking**
:^y	**Talking**
C(_)~	**Teapot**
C(_)~'	**Teapot**
:`-(	**Tear**
:\'-)	**Tear of Happiness**
&-|	**Tearful**
:p	**Teasing**
(((((^_^)	**Teleporting**
-(:)(0)=8	**Teletubby**
:-)---	**Thin as a Pin**
$-)	**Thinking About Money**
\m/	**This Rocks**
:-)</////>	**Tie**
[]---|<O---[]	**Tight Rope**
(:|	**Tired**
%-|	**Tired**
2B|^2B	**To Be or Not To Be**
0000(0)(0)0000	**Toes**
l,lO	**Toilet**
:-Q	**Tongue Hanging Out in Disgust**
:-J	**Tongue in Cheek**
-)	**Tongue In Cheek**
:-?	**Tongue In Cheek**
:- ?	**Tongue Sticking Out**
:-&	**Tongue Tied**
:-a	**Tongue Touching Nose**
[|:)	**Top Hat**
!#!^*&:-	**Total Head Case**
#:o\:o/:o\:o/:o||	**Totem Pole**
}(:-(	**Toupee Blowing in Wind**
{:-)	**Toupee Smile**
-HHHH	**Tower**

---(o_ _)o	Tripping
ₒₒ(o_ _)o⌒☆	Tripping
(>_<)>	Troubled
(^_^;)	Troubled
oo---oo-Bo	Truck
-=iii=<()	Trumpet
O>-O>-|-<O-<O	Tug of War
@=)	Turban
<:>==	Turkey
/Y\	Tuxedo
:-)8---	Tuxedo
:-)8>	Tuxedo
(-::-(	Two-faced

"Letter U"

=-O	"Uh-oh"
(o|o)	Ultraman
(um)	Umbrella
(---,	Umbrella
x:-/	Uncertain
=):-)	Uncle Sam
=):-)>	Uncle Sam
:-\	Undecided
:\	Undecided
/:-|	Undecided
_(*-*)_/	
|	Undecided
/\	
:-|	Unfazed
:<	Unhappy
:-c	Unhappy
<:-)	Unibrow
|:-)	Unibrow
|:	Unimpressed
**==	United States Flag

:-t	Unsmiley
(:-	Unsmiley
(:-(	Unsmiley
:-[	Unsmiling
>->'	Unsure
|:-|	Unyielding
>.<	Upset
}:(	Upset
>:*	Upset
D:<	Upset
>=P	Upset
.-.	Upside Down
P:	Upward Lick
^URS	Up Yours

"Letter V"

:-[	Vampire
:-E	Vampire
(';.;')	Vampire
@,..,@	Vampire
,..,	Vampire
-,..,-	Vampire
^,..,^	Vampire
:-{	Vampire
:f	Vampire
',..,'	Vampire
(0,..,0)	Vampire
(=,..,=)	Vampire
^,..,^	Vampire Bat
(^-^:)	Vampire Bite
%*}	Very Drunk
:-))))	Very Happy
=D	Very Happy
:-((	Very Sad
%')	Very Tired

(:-(	Very Unhappy
8Ö<	Video Projector
](-[3	Viking
:O=	Vomit

"Letter W"

(>'.')>#	Waffle
(>'_')>#	Waffle
#<(0.0<)	Waffle
:->X==|	Waiter
:-w	Waiting
:-<	Walrus
:3=	Walrus
(:{C)	Walrus
(:3=	Walrus
._)	Warping
:-h	Wave
~~c___	Waves
(^_^)／	Waving
@:-)	Wavy Hair
:-)--	Weakling
{(:-)	Wearing a Toupee
[:-)	Wearing a Walkman
8-)	Wearing Contacts
B-)	Wearing Glasses
:-{}	Wearing Lipstick
]-I	Wearing Sunglasses
{:-)	Wears a Toupee
('~`)	Weary
;-(	Weeping
:|=.===.=|: \ O / | _/_	Weightlifting
:-s	What?!

185

:>	What?
:@	What?
:-P	Whatever
-_-	Whatever
:-1	Whatever
(¬_¬)	Whatever
#:-S	Whew
:'(	Whining
:'-(	Whining
:-"	Whistling
.'Y	Whistling
8)	Wide-Eyed, Wears Glasses
8-|	Wide-Eyed Surprised
;^?	Wigged Out
(w)	Wilted Rose
())=(	Wine Glass
;p	Wink
;-P	Wink
;^)	Wink
(`_^)	Wink
,-)	Wink
(^_~)	Wink
9-)	Wink
6-)	Wink
;-)	Winking
~_^	Winking
;()	Winking
'-)	Winking
;)	Winking smile
;-D	Winking & Laughing
\')	Winky
\'-)	Winky
^_^a	Wiping Tears
<):^/	Witch
<|:~,	Witch

I8$\{\}	**Witch Doctor**
<\{\{\};->~	**Wizard**
<*(:-?	**Wizard**
-=#:-)	**Wizard**
8<:-)	**Wizard**
\{0-|<[	**Woman**
o>-<|=	**Woman**
:-)8 :	**Woman**
o.o?	**Wondering**
:~)	**Wondering**
:-S	**Worried**
(——;)	**Worried**
8-]	**Wow!**
%-|	**Work Late**
:-/	**Wry Face**
:-i	**Wry Smile**
\}-)	**Wry Smile**
,-\}	**Wry and Winking**

"Letter X"

8==8O8==8	**X-Wing**
>8\{\}8<:	**X-Wing**
(xx)	**Xbox**
[x]	**Xbox**

"Letter Y"

_/)	**Yacht**
:-o	**Yawn**
|-O	**Yawning**
|^o	**Yawning or Snoring variation**
\o/	**Yay**
:-0	**Yell**
:-(0)	**Yelling**
=8-0	**Yikes!**
(%)	**Yin Yang**

<(-_-)>	Yoda
<(-.-)>	Yoda
>=^ p	Yuck
8-p	Yuck!
:-0>	Yuck Face
$-)	Yuppie

"Letter Z"

Z	Zorro
F(x_x)F	Zombie
8-#	Zombie
B-)===>	ZZ Top